Theology Today
41 Salvation and Damnation

Theology Today

GENERAL EDITOR:
EDWARD YARNOLD, S.J.

No. 41

Salvation and Damnation

BY

WILLIAM J. DALTON, S.J.

distributed by
CLERGY BOOK SERVICE
BUTLER, WISCONSIN

ISBN-0-85342-524-8

Nihil Obstat:
Mgr. Francis Thomas, S.T.L.
Birmingham, 12th July 1977

Imprimatur:
Mgr. D. Leonard, V.G.
Birmingham, 12th July 1977

Cum licentia superiorum ordinis

TO YOUNG

JESUIT BROTHERS

WHO BELIEVE THAT

PERFECT LOVE

CASTS OUT FEAR

ACKNOWLEDGEMENT

The Scripture quotations in this publication are taken from the *Revised Standard Version of the Bible* copyrighted 1946 and 1952 by the Division of Christian Education of the National Council of the Churches of Christ in the U.S.A. and used by kind permission.

ABBREVIATION

Dz H. Denzinger and A. Schonmetzer, *Enchiridion Symbolorum, Definitionum et Declarationum* (33rd edit., Barcelona etc., 1965).

CONTENTS

PREFACE

Most Christians must at some time or other have asked themselves what heaven would be like if someone dear to them were in hell. One answer could be that in heaven we shall see the rightness of God's will, so that the fact that he condemns someone to eternal punishment will not detract from the joy of heaven. Another answer is that we know that there is a hell, but we do not know if there is anyone in it. A third answer is that since the life after death is a grace, not a natural sequel to this life, there is no reason to believe that God would continue the life of anyone simply in order to punish him; hell is annihilation. A fourth view is that hell is more like purgatory, offering the chance of eventual salvation.

Father Dalton's suggestion is more radical. Examining the New Testament texts he suggests that, while all language about the after-life is metaphorical, the metaphors about heaven work in a different way from those about hell. Heaven is an eternal state, though we cannot conceive what it is like; whereas hell, though a possibility for all, is one from which Christ, by his death and resurrection, has rescued everybody. God's will to save *all* human beings, which is so central to the gospel message, will somehow be fulfilled.

E. J. Yarnold, S.J.

INTRODUCTION

In March 1965, Charles Davis wrote: 'The question must be faced: where does hell fit into the Good News?' ('The Thought of Hell', *America* 112 [1965], p. 394). Ten years afterwards, one can still ask, 'Where indeed?' At the time, the beginnings of an answer which Davis provided in his short article, 'The Thought of Hell', seemed satisfactory. He firmly rejected one solution, 'the refusal to envisage the genuine possibility of hell in the present order'. He rejected with equal firmness another view, 'that most men are damned, the saved being plucked from the mass of men hurtling down the road to hell.' Without entering into the mystery of the number of the saved, Davis saw in 'the serious possibility of damnation' an essential element of Christian revelation.

I am not so sure, now, that this answer is really satisfactory. At least it is open to discussion. One can ask about whom we are talking, 'sinners' or, very personally, myself. One can ask too what is the meaning of the phrase, 'serious possibility'. Must I give a statistical probability, no matter how slight, to my own damnation? Of course we cannot expect to arrive at a dogmatic conclusion that all men are saved; but we can ask whether there are well founded theological reasons for thinking that this is the case.

Again, does human freedom demand, for every man, the real possibility of damnation? If so, was Jesus, the man, free? Or must we suppose, in his case also, the possibility of damnation? Hopefully, one is not tempted to find a way out by doubting his real humanity! And, if it is argued that the case of Jesus is altogether special, since the New Testament bears witness to his utter sinlessness, what are we to make of the Catholic tradition that the apostles were confirmed in grace? Without arguing for or against the fact, one ought to admit that the very idea of such a confirmation does not seem to contradict legitimate human freedom. Could we not suppose that God, who created men in love and wisdom, would keep them *human*, with that minimum of moral goodness which is necessary for a truly human condition? If a man ends his life not totally bad, with some glimmerings of real human love, then dare we exclude from God the power to develop this into eternal life? But if, on the contrary, one imagines or seems to find human beings totally wicked, one can still ask to what degree such a person is really responsible, to what degree he is sick or helpless. God may well be more merciful than the average righteous Christian.

Again, in traditional Christian theology, it is accepted that all those who are finally saved are saved precisely because God willed to save them by his grace (Dz 625, etc.). They are not saved partly because of God's grace and partly because of their right exercise of free will. It is not our business to discuss here how this is to be theologically explained. The point is that, in Christian tradition, there is place for a legitimate predestination which does not do violence to human freedom. Further, it is also the teaching of the Catholic Church that final perseverance in grace is a special grace of God which cannot be merited by even the holiest of lives (Dz 832). One may ask, then, why this predestination should not be extended, despite human freedom and weakness, to all men.

On another plane, can I, as a believing Christian, seriously envisage the possibility of my own damnation? If so, on what do I found my hope of salvation? In Christ's great love for me? Unfortunately this great love must cope with my weak and sinful self if I am to be saved. The weak line in the chain of my salvation is precisely this fragile and unpredictable me. Despite Christ's great love, I can always say 'No'. Will I perversely and finally reject this love? Who knows? There are examples around me of people who, for one reason or another, apparently fall away. What, then, becomes of Christian hope? Am I not bound in servitude to a life of agonizing fear, not fear of God so much as fear of myself?

It is true that the Council of Trent taught, against the Protestant reformers, that no one without a special revelation from God could be absolutely and infallibly sure of his own final salvation (Dz 826): but it may well be asked if the problematic of Trent is precisely that we are discussing. Catholic theologians would admit that a Christian may be *practically* sure of his own salvation, always accepting this as a grace (See K. Rahner, H. Vorgrimler, *Theological Dictionary*, 'Certainty of Salvation', pp. 70-71). Nor was the problem of hell raised at the time of the Reformation. Both Protestants and Catholics were untroubled at the thought of vast numbers of people, particularly heretics, Jews and infidels, being consigned to eternal torments. Within its frame of reference, the statement of Trent could be accepted: it insisted on the freedom of men under God's grace. But, if the doctrine of hell in fact needs to be reinterpreted, then it is obvious that adjustments will have to be made all along the line of Church statements about man's ultimate destiny. Scripture scholars are quite used to the re-interpretation of biblical texts in the light of better understanding of literary and historical background; systematic theologians will have to be prepared to do the same for their sacred texts in Christian tradition.

Let us suppose that I take heart from my faith in the God of love and power and from my experience of his grace in my life, that I stoutly assert with Paul that nothing can separate me, the believer, from the love of God in Christ Jesus, our Lord (Rom 8.39). But, if I can say this for myself, without being able to sound in my own person the mystery of sin still present in me, what right have I to hold hell open to other men? God alone knows what goes on in the depth of their hearts and mine. Like me, they all show in their lives the radical presence of good and evil. If God can find any real good there, can he not, the almighty Lord of love, develop this into eternal life? And let us give up our useless and presumptuous practice of pointing to particular men as evil and fit for hell — Hitler is a favourite example. Only God can tell where, in any particular man, freedom begins, where sickness begins, where good can be found, where evil. We too easily forget the story of Jesus about the Pharisee and the tax collector.

Even if we push the possibility of hell back into the mystery of God, the transcendent and almight God of Job who refuses to enter into discussion with our petty theologizing, the thought of losing any brother or sister of mine in hell is intolerable. Never were thinking and sensitive people so aware as now of the brotherhood of man. This is surely the work of grace. In the global village of today I see and feel that what happens to any man happens to me. I am more aware than ever before that I am in fact my brother's keeper. He belongs to me and I to him. One may well ask, 'Can any man in the history of mankind be really and fully saved if all men are not saved?'

Men of religious feeling, when they look around at the sin and evil of the world, often think that somehow justice must be done, that there must be some form of final retribution to pay back to the sinner the terrible consequences of his evil which are only too apparent in human life. C. F. D. Moule has tackled this problem in a number of recent articles, one of which can be particularly recommended: 'The Theology of Forgiveness', to be found in the book, *From Faith to Faith, Studies of Suffering and Wholeness*, pp. 61-72 (ed. Norman Hutton, London, 1971). He finds that the basic teaching of the New Testament does not support such a view: 'on the personal level, the motive of forgiveness is always to heal and restore the offender and never "to take it out on him" by punishment or reprisals or retaliation' (p. 66). We would do well to forget the requirements of abstract justice and to put ourselves and all men in the hands of God, whose powers of forgiveness are startling because they are beyond all human comprehension. It does not follow that forgiveness is easy, easy for God in Jesus Christ or easy for the sinner. We are all dimly aware of the possibilities of our self-inflicted blindness. The question is whether we may firmly hope, for ourselves and for others, that mercy and light will prevail.

Davis refers in his article to the silence about hell in preaching and popular religious writing. I myself have asked a variety of believing and practising Christians how the doctrine of hell fits into their life of faith. In many cases, it does not fit in at all; in fact, it has been largely forgotten. The quick conclusion that such people are deficient in their understanding of the

Christian faith or too lax in responding to the severe demands of the gospel is not necessarily the correct one. The Holy Spirit falls on the whole Church, not merely on official Church leaders. Could it be that the disappearance of hell from the lives of such people, who give every evidence of living the positive aspects of the gospel, is a sign that we need a new and radically different interpretation of hell? Perhaps the hell of the past might well disappear.

Does all this demand too violent a departure from the doctrine which our Christian ancestors simply accepted? Again, before offering a quick reply, we might look to parallels from the past. The formula, 'Outside the Church there is no salvation', is too sacred to be deleted from our theological treatises; but how different is the meaning we give to it now from that believed and proclaimed in the Church in former times! Yet, in those times, the more narrow and exclusive interpretation of the dictum seemed to be securely based on the word of the New Testament itself. Here a better understanding of the literary and historical background of the New Testament led scholars to see the limitations of scriptural statements which seemed to be absolute. To the superficial reader what is more absolute than: 'Unless one is born of water and the Spirit, he cannot enter the kingdom of God' (Jn 3.5)? Today there are still many who feel bound to defend the hard and unpopular doctrine of hell because it is clearly stated in the New Testament. In other areas we have learnt to distrust verbal citations of Scripture as a basis for Christian life and belief, even when these citations are accurately repeated in the traditional formulas of the Church. Could we not allow that the Holy Spirit in our times may be calling us to take a new look at the message of the New Testament, to move beyond the apparent statements about eternal perdition to a better understanding of the good news as it is meant for the sinful, wayward, unreliable sons of God?

It is possible that the doctrine of hell as officially proposed in the Church, with its threat of eternal torture, has turned out something of an over-kill and has come to be dismissed by many people as simply unacceptable. Hell might be taken more seriously if it were seen as a symbol of the incompatibility of sin with the all-holy God. It still remains true that for every sinner and to the degree that he is a sinner 'it is a fearful thing to fall into the hands of the living God' (Heb 10.31). Sin must somehow be destroyed in a man before he can live in harmony with his God. Our imagination fails us when we try to picture this final situation, but we have every reason to think of this purification as a profound and searing experience. If there be any human being who thinks he can stroll into the presence of the Almighty with the corruption of selfishness still deep within him, he is destined to a rude and shattering awakening. But what we must discuss very earnestly is whether men, according to the teaching of the Church, have to face the hazard of *eternal* punishment, an *eternity* of absolute misery and failure.

These are serious questions. It is the aim of this work to return to the sources of Christian revelation in the Scriptures, to see something of the development of the doctrine of hell in Christian thought and, finally, to attempt to formulate some conclusions. It would be too much to expect quick and easy answers. Even if the questions remain, to a great extent, unanswered, it is hoped that a step, even a small step, may be taken on the way to a better understanding of what the good news of salvation may mean to the Christian of today.

Chapter I

OLD TESTAMENT AND JEWISH BACKGROUND

It is not to our purpose to discuss fully the Old Testament views of the after-life. It is generally asserted that the thrust of the Old Testament is solidly directed towards this present life. In keeping with their near eastern neighbours, the people of Israel did believe in some form of after-life, so weakened and dim as scarcely to be called human, in a realm often called Sheol. Here men survive in chaotic darkness (Job 10.21-22), in silence (Ps 94.17), without knowledge of God (Ps 88.6); they are weary (Job 3.17), lacking in strength (Ps 88.4). It is important to note that this condition of the dead has nothing to do with the good or evil of their earthly lives. Hence, this topic, interesting though it be of itself, has nothing to do with our present investigation, which is concerned with retribution.

However it should be pointed out that in recent times this prevalent opinion about Israel's concept of the after-life has been challenged by M. Dahood (see his third volume on the Psalms, published in 1969, in the Anchor Bible series, pp. XL1-L11). He insists that there is clear evidence in the Proverbs (14.32; 16.2; 15.24) that the writer expected final salvation after death. Basing his interpretation upon Ugaritic texts, which he maintains are fundamentally important for the study of ancient Hebrew poetry, he gives many examples, particularly from the Psalms and Proverbs, where 'life' should be translated 'eternal life', where 'future' implies a future beyond the grave, where the banquet which God provides for the good man is in God's eternity. He finds examples of what later theology would call the beatific vision, and other expressions implying a life beyond the grave. The vast majority of these texts deal with the destiny of the good man, but a few of them (e.g., Ps 37.38; 69.29; 109.13; Prov 24.20) deal with the fate of the wicked.

The debate among Old Testament scholars will no doubt go on for some time before anything like a consensus of opinion emerges about the interpretation of these texts. Meanwhile, it is still commonly asserted that only in Hellenistic times do we find the beginnings of a doctrine of punishment in the after-life. In the Book of Enoch, the fate of the wicked after death is clearly different from that of the dead in general (10.2; 22; 102.5). This view emerges with great clarity in the Book of Wisdom (accepted in Roman Catholic tradition as canonical scripture). Here man, as he comes from God's hand, is declared imperishable (2.23). While the souls of the good are at peace in the presence of God (3.1-2), the wicked at death will be dis-honoured (4.19), will face God's terrible judgment (4.20), at which the utter futility of their earthly lives will be revealed (5.4-13). The fate and punishment of sinners is described in terms of the great apocalyptic battle: the whole universe will become the instrument of God's punishment (5.17-23). There is no further speculation about their future.

Belief in the resurrection of the body brings a new element into the concept of the after-life. Here again we are dealing with a large topic of great interest, which we shall have to be content to touch briefly within the limits of our study. Despite possible references to the resurrection of the body in earlier texts of the Old Testament (e.g., Is 26.19; Job 19.25-27; Ps 17.15), it is commonly accepted that the first clear statement comes in Dan 12.2: 'Many of those who sleep in the dust of the earth shall awake, some to everlasting life, and some to shame and everlasting contempt.' As the text stands, it seems to refer to Israelites only. This limited form of resurrection was common in later Jewish writings; in fact, one popular view was that, while all souls will be summoned to judgment, only the righteous will be raised to a new life. Again, there were different views about the implications of this new life: some writers looked forward to a bodily resur-rection, others to a purely spiritual existence. Thus, in the Book of Enoch, we find both traditions, that of the resur-rection of the body in 1-36, 62.14 and 83-90, that of the resurrection of the soul in 91-94.

In 2 Macc 7, the future resurrection to eternal life of the heroic martyrs is envisaged: their bodily sufferings imply a bodily resurrection. The cruel tyrant will face a stern judgment, but his fate is not further specified. In 2 Macc 12.38-45, we have an interesting situation. Some of the Jewish soldiers who had fallen in battle were discovered to have sinned in taking with them idol amulets. Judas had money collected for a sacrifice to be offered for them in the Temple, thus bearing witness to his belief in the resurrection from the dead. Thus the Jews who took part in the holy war were regarded as eligible for resurrection. Nothing is said about the fate of the fallen soldiers, if sacrifices and prayers had not been offered for them. Nor is there any hint about the lot of the wicked after death.

In non-canonical Jewish literature, the term Gehenna (Valley of Hinnom) began to be used to describe the place of the damned. This was a deep valley to the south of Jerusalem, where in pre-exilic times Moloch worship took place. It was ritually desecrated by Josiah (2 Kgs 23.10), but to little effect, since in the time of Jeremiah it again became the scene of idolatrous rites (Jer 7.31-32; 19.2-6; 32.35). It was then declared by the prophet 'the valley of slaughter', since in it the Jews fleeing Jerusalem would be killed and there they would lie unburied (Jer 7.32; 19.6).

No doubt there is a reference to this same tradition in Is 66.24: 'And they shall go forth and look at the dead bodies of the men that have rebelled against me; for the worm shall not die, the fire shall not be quenched, and they shall be an abhorrence of all flesh.' This description must be taken more as an imaginative presentation of utter horror than a theological statement about hell (cf. Mk 9.48).

These ideas are developed in later writings (e.g., Enoch 26.1 27.3), and, in due course, the locality of Gehenna was forgotten; it became simply the place of final punishment for the wicked. While in some accounts this punishment was reserved until the final judgment at the last day, in other accounts, particularly those deriving from the Pharisees, the torment of the wicked began immediately after death (Josephus, *Ant.*, XVIII, 1:3; *War*, II, 8:14). A common tradition set the place of damnation under the earth, and, in the mind of some writers, the original Valley of Hinnom became one of the gates to hell.

In the Jewish apocalyptic writings, imagination runs riot in the description of hell. For example, in the Book of the Secrets of Enoch it is a place of complete darkness with every possible torture: river of fire, icy cold, where the inmates suffer both from cruel thirst and shivering (10.2-3). The guardians of Gehenna suit the place: they are like 'serpents, and their faces like lamps that have gone out, their eyes like darkened flames, and their teeth bare down to their breast' (42.1). In this understanding of hell there are no gradations: all the wicked are in the same situation. They cannot be helped by relatives or friends; they cannot repent; their suffering is all the greater because they see the joy of the saved (2 Esdras 7.101-105; 2 Baruch 85.12-13).

Later rabbis were repelled by the savagery of the hell envisaged by apocalyptic writers. Eternal punishment was limited to a very few special cases of notorious sin. Lesser sinners were released after a time. In the more lenient school of Hillel, twelve months was the maximum penalty for all but the most hardened sinners. It was understood that no Jew could be so wicked as to incur this maximum. Sinners in Gehenna could be helped by the prayers of those on earth and, in any case, they were granted respite from their sufferings on the Sabbath day. There were rabbis who could not accept eternal punishment even for the most notorious sinners: These would finally be released or completely destroyed. And finally a very merciful opinion exempted from the pains of Gehenna all those who suffered severely in this life, from poverty, ill health, or even from an unhappy marriage (*The Universal Jewish Encyclopedia*, art. 'Gehinnom', p. 521).

While it is difficult to date precisely the religious views expressed in the many Jewish writings of the time, it is clear that there was a wide variety of opinion about future retribution in the Jewish world before Christ. This may come as a surprise to Christians who take the New Testament picture as the only Jewish view. In the New Testament, hell is mentioned often enough, but there is little speculation about its nature.

Clearly the severer view is supposed. One may well ask if the more stringent understanding of hell is part of Christian revelation or simply an element of Jewish background accepted uncritically and without discussion. There is certainly no evidence that the New Testament writers selected their view of hell from among many others as that precisely demanded by Christian revelation. We have no opportunity of asking Jesus or Paul or the other dominant figures about their final and considered views on retribution. We have to make a critical and historical judgment as to what place this religious furniture, inherited from one stream of the past, held in their total message. After all, the gospel is *good* news, news of salvation. The implications of the gospel did not appear all at once. For example, Paul, despite his magnificent understanding of the gospel, did not see that slavery, as an institution, was radically incompatible with it. Is it possible that a too literal clinging to the text of the New Testament has prevented an opening up of its message to illuminate man's ultimate destiny? Paul broke up the exclusiveness which separated Jew from pagan, freeman from slave, men from women. Is it time for us to question the final exclusiveness by which we too easily separate the good from the bad, the saved from the damned?

Chapter II

HELL IN THE NEW TESTAMENT

The Problem

In this section we shall discuss those elements in the New Testament which bear on the doctrine of hell. All later theological reflections and definitions take the teaching of the New Testament as a basis; hence the importance of this section cannot be overestimated. There seem to be two streams of tradition, both authenticated in New Testament writings: that of judgment, of condemnation, of eternal rejection of the unrepentant sinner, and, on the other hand, that of salvation founded on the precisely Christian understanding of God as the creator and supreme lover of all men and all things, whose will is to save and whose will is inevitably fulfilled. There is no easy solution to this problem; and the solution is certainly not to be found in counting and juxtaposing texts. It requires an effort of interpretation which will do justice at once to the text of the New Testament and to the tradition of faith in the Church.

Of the two themes, that of judgment and that of salvation, it might be thought that the former was so evident that it should dominate the interpretation of the latter. Thus one could say that it is evident from the New Testament that God condemns (or could condemn) certain persons to eternal punishment, and that the statements of apparently universal salvation found in other texts must be adjusted to suit the demands of the doctrine of judgment.

However, one may wonder whether such a method of putting the two themes side by side and letting them, as it were, fight the matter out is the correct one. First of all, the Christian God is primarily a saving God: 'the Son of man came to seek and to save the lost' (Lk 19.10). Secondly, the presentation of salvation and of judgment are at different levels. The term salvation is an analogical application to God of a human activity; it expresses man's need for God if he is to achieve his full destiny. But this analogy is at once more direct and in less need of interpretation than the term judgment. The judge, after all, in human society is an official bounded by the very limitations of that society. When this term is applied to God, great care must be taken not to form an image of God in the likeness of man. Thus, for this reason also, it would seem more suitable to start with the theme of salvation and later, with some effort at correct interpretation, to discuss the theme of judgment.

Salvation

Is there any evidence in the New Testament to suggest that God not only wishes to save all men but that he will actually do so?

At first sight, this seems an odd question. Surely if God wishes something to happen, this effect will be produced. One obvious comment might be that God respects human freedom and that salvation *also* depends on the free co-operation of the individual man. But here we have to avoid the mistake of putting God and man side by side, with God endeavouring to persuade and man assenting or dissenting. It is not to our purpose here to discuss at depth the enormous problem which has so baffled theologians of the past, namely, the conciliation of two ideas seemingly opposed, that of God's supreme power and that of man's free will. Here at least one important point can be made. God acts within the human person: because he is transcendent he can and does act immanently. Although the problem remains, one can at least move a step towards understanding how God's power and man's freedom can be harmonized. A further ramification of this problem would be the question of how man can sin at all — but this is beyond the scope of our discussion. At the moment let it suffice to cite a text from Paul which lies at the heart of our problem: 'For God has consigned all men to disobedience, that he may have mercy upon all' (Rom 11.32). Here we are simply asking whether God's desire that all should be *finally* saved is inevitably fulfilled without denying the freedom and responsibility of man.

We might start with the general biblical picture of God and his relationship with men. From the beginning of his revelation to Israel, he is presented as the saving God. Of course, equally from the beginning he is the God who judges, but there is a certain evolution. At first we have a fierce exclusivism, centred in the idea of a chosen people, but later, as for example in the moving end of Jonah, God is seen as the God who loves and saves all men, even the Ninevites:

> And the Lord said, 'You pity the plant for which you did not labour, nor did you make it grow, which came into being in a night, and perished in a night. And should I not pity Nineveh, that great city, in which there are more than a hundred and twenty thousand persons who do not know their right hand from their left, and also much cattle?' (Jon 4.10-11).

Finally, in the New Testament God is seen realising through Christ the fulfillment of his plan of salvation. Now his salvation penetrates deep into the being of man, deep into his future, so that man now, through faith, can be totally saved. And this very faith is seen to be the gift of God, not merely a correct exercise of human free will. Given the communitarian nature of man, his brotherly union with all other men, it may well be asked whether this total salvation should not be also total in extent, including every human being who has ever lived. In this way, in God's final salvation, no brother would have to mourn the loss of his brother and for no one would Christ have finally died in vain.

Paul

Such ideas seem to be supported by a number of New Testament texts. Would it be possible to find in the text cited above an emphatic summing up of Paul's theology, a sort of first principle of God's economy of salvation? 'God has consigned all men to disobedience, so that he may have mercy upon all.'

Note where the passage comes in Paul's argument. Paul certainly does not underrate sin. His powerful exposition of the sins of pagans and Jews is developed in Chs. 1-3. It is against the setting of sin that he presents his stirring picture of salvation in Christ through faith (3.21-31; 5.1-11; 8.1-39). Finally, he deals with the problem of the unbelief of the Jews, discerning even here the mystery of God's love. God is seen, despite the sins of men, even through the sins of men, to be a saving God. And so Paul can end with an exclamation of wonder at God's mercy and wisdom: 'O the depths of the riches and wisdom and knowledge of God! How unsearchable are his judgments and how inscrutable his ways!' (11.33).

Karl Barth, in his commentary on Romans (*The Epistle to the Romans*, London, 1933), gives lyrical expression of his appreciation of this sentence. It is for him the key to all Paul's theological thought. In fact, every reader faces in this text a fundamental challenge: by it he is judged. Here he encounters 'the hidden, unknown, incomprehensible God, to whom nothing is impossible, the Lord, who is as such our Father in Jesus Christ.' We are indeed invited to stretch our small minds and hearts and imaginations to take in a glimpse of God's magnificent forgiveness.

Commentators find it hard to make this effort. They have various ways of trimming the text down to more manageable proportions. In the context, it can be said, Paul is thinking of God's providence in the conversion to the faith of Gentiles and Jews. He is not concerned with the individual salvation of all men, but only of groups; these groups are to be taken in their historical progress. It can be urged, too, that not all men of the past, whether Jew or Gentile, were guilty of the moral aberrations described in Rom 1.18-3.20. So we could conclude, by a sort of parallel, that not all individuals, including Gentiles and Jews, will reach final salvation.

While Paul's thought is certainly global, this is not to say that logically it excludes the destiny of individuals. Each and every individual is depicted as estranged from God: this is the point of Paul's long denunciation of Gentile and Jewish aberrations. All men need the saving grace of Christ. In fact, Paul can see in transgressions of the law (and this includes law in the widest sense, not merely the Jewish Law) an opportunity for the sinner to come to his senses, to realize his state of need. Thus he can say:

> What then shall we say? That the law is sin? By no
> means. Yet if it had not been for the law, I should not
> have known sin . . . But sin, finding opportunity in the
> commandment, deceived me and by it killed me . . . It
> was sin, working death in me through what is good, in
> order that sin might be shown to be sin, and through the
> commandment might become sinful beyond measure
> (Rom 7.7a,11,13b,14).

It is sin, *hamartia*, lying underneath the transgressions, revealing itself in transgressions, which was universal. This is the
fundamental estrangement from God which cannot be identi-
fied with any particular moral aberration. How one under-
stands this estrangement depends on one's theology of sin; but
certainly in the mind of Paul, this sin is universal, and secondly, a condition of human life which underlies what we would
call 'actual sins'.

Similarly, in the mind of Paul, salvation is not a matter of
virtuous actions. It is a free gift of God, of which, no doubt,
virtuous actions are the fruit and sign. Thus, one might conclude from Rom 11.32 that literally all men receive from God
this salvation in its fullest and final sense. This is the view of
such an objective scholar as Dodd who finds in the text 'a
complete redintegration of the human race'.

Paul's earlier treatment of justification and salvation tends
to support this view:

> But now the righteousness of God has been manifested
> apart from the law . . . the righteousness of God through
> faith in Jesus Christ for all who believe. For there is no
> distinction; since all have sinned and fall short of the
> glory of God, they are justified by his grace as a gift,
> through the redemption which is in Christ Jesus (Rom
> 3.21-24).

Paul's hope takes him beyond justification to final salvation:

> Through him we have obtained access to this grace in
> which we stand, and we rejoice in our hope of sharing
> the glory of God . . . Since, therefore, we are now justi-
> fied by his blood, much more shall we be saved by him
> from the wrath of God (Rom 5.2,9).

It can be seen that there are elements in the theology of Paul which would seem to favour the final salvation of all men. Yet Paul himself speaks in a limited context. He is primarily concerned with the destiny of those who believe the message of the gospel and who accept the gift of faith, realising that the very acceptance comes under the gift: the Christian cannot boast even of the 'work' of his acceptance, but only of the gift of God. Paul is not thinking directly of those who have never heard the gospel preached or of those to whom the gospel has not been adequately presented. Elsewhere he speaks of the judgment of those who do not accept the gospel:

> And even if our gospel is veiled, it is veiled only to those who are perishing. In their case the god of this world has blinded the minds of the unbelievers, to keep them from seeing the light of the gospel of the glory of Christ, who is the likeness of God (2 Cor 4:3-4).

Of this judgment we shall have much to say later on.

But the question can still be asked: Do the principles of justification and salvation proposed by Paul logically imply some way of implicit faith in those who have never heard the gospel message or who have never had this message adequately proposed? Certainly in Rom 2.14-16 Paul seems to describe a way to God possible for the pagans who lived before the time of Christ; it seems logical to suppose that those pagans who, even after the coming of Christ, have no means of reaching him by explicit faith in him, would not be in a worse situation than those before his coming. Even for those who hear the gospel message and culpably reject it, could not this refusal be looked on as a form of 'transgression' permitted by God only that finally, even in the case of the individual, his grace might triumph?

There is one important point of interpretation to be kept in mind. In his letter to the Romans, Paul's theology has two aspects. In one he moves in the history of salvation. This salvation was promised to Abraham's posterity, but God retained his sovereign freedom in interpreting this promise. Thus, apart from any merits of Jacob and Esau, it was Jacob and his descendants who were chosen by God. And of these descendants it was the prophetic 'remnant' who were again chosen, that is, those Jews who were converted to Christ. Beyond this Paul foresees the conversion of the pagans and finally 'all Israel will be saved' (chs 9-11). But underneath this historical approach, there is a second and more fundamental aspect which in Paul's thought is dialectical, that is, transcending the limitations of history. All men, both before and after Christ, are sinners; all men, whatever their period of history, are called to conversion, faith and salvation. Abraham was justified by faith (ch. 4) and even pagans, who stood outside the divine promise, are not excluded from salvation (2.7-10, 14-16). Thus, when we come to the central affirmation of 11.32, 'God has consigned all men to disobedience, in order that he may have mercy on all', we are justified in seeing here a statement not merely about the future, that in due course pagans and Jews, in some representative totality, will enter the Christian church, but a general statement affecting all mankind from the beginning to the end of human history. Paul has never indicated how precisely those who have never heard of Christ can be saved by faith and by Christ; but it would be doing injustice to his thought if we were to limit his sphere of salvation to some chosen Jews and to the present and future members of the Christian church. The emphatic 'all', which dominates the first eleven chapters of Romans, should be given its full value.

In the same way, in his famous comparison between Adam and Christ in 5.12-21, Paul appears to be thinking historically, beginning with Adam, dealing with the period before Moses, the time after Moses, the coming of Christ and his salvation. But here too his fundamental thought is dialectical. All men, of all times, share the sin which had its origin with Adam. To all men is offered the grace of salvation in Christ. This is the way we should understand another powerful statement: 'For as by one man's disobedience many have been made sinners, so by one man's obedience many will be made righteous' (5.19).

A similar universalist doctrine seems to be supposed in texts in the Pauline tradition: 'For in him all the fullness of God was pleased to dwell, and through him to reconcile to himself all things, whether on earth or in heaven, making peace by the blood of his cross' (Col 1:19-20). Similarly we read in Eph 1.10: 'For he has made known to us in all wisdom and insight the mystery of his will, according to his purpose which he set forth in Christ as a plan for the fullness of time, to unite all things to him, things in heaven and things on earth.' Again one may ask, if it is God's will to unite, to reconcile to himself the whole universe in Christ, whether this reconciliation should not extend to all men. This optimistic view seems to be supported by the picture of the end in 1 Cor 15.24-26,28:

> Then comes the end, when he delivers the kingdom to God the Father after destroying every rule and every authority and power. For he must reign until he has put all his enemies under his feet. The last enemy to be destroyed is death . . . When all things are subjected to him, then the Son himself will also be subjected to him who put all things under him, that God may be everything to every one.

The destruction of 'death', which in Pauline terminology does not mean merely physical death but also spiritual death, seems to imply that, at the end, nowhere in God's creation will there be the discordant note of sin, but that complete peace and harmony will reign. It is hard to see how this picture will be fulfilled if, for all eternity, there could be a number of human beings who reject God and remain alienated from him.

Other Texts

In the rest of the New Testament, while no doubt it is assumed that Jesus Christ is, in some way, the saviour of all men, there is little to indicate that he will, in fact, save all men. We do have the remarkable text of Jn 12.31-32: 'Now is the judgment of this world, now shall the ruler of this world be cast out; and I, when I am lifted up from the earth, will draw all men to myself.' Here the 'ruler of this world' and the world are judged, but the human beings who had belonged to the world in so far as they were subject to the devil, these will be drawn to the Son of Man (See the comment on this text in E.C. Hoskyns, *The Fourth Gospel*, 2nd ed., London, 1947). It is certainly no just comment on this passage to say with Buis

(*The Doctrine of Eternal Punishment*, Philadelphia, 1957, pp. 113-114) that 'it is not stated what Christ will do with men when he draws them to himself: he may condemn them!' Elsewhere in the gospel we read: 'No one can come to me unless the Father who sent me draws him' (Jn 6.44). 'Coming to Jesus', 'being drawn by the Son of man lifted up', 'being drawn by the Father', all these mean believing in Jesus and sharing eternal life. At least we may say that, if the full universal import of 12.32 is to be watered down, then this needs to be justified.

Again, even when we seem to have reference elsewhere to eternal damnation, as in the case of Judas, 'the son of perdition' (17.12), we have the right to ask if this is rather an apparent contradiction than a real one. It is at least possible that Christian tradition has been a little too ready to find satisfaction in the eternal punishment of Judas, whereas the actual text leaves the matter a good deal more vague. One can ask whether we have the right to make more explicit what the text leaves mysterious. As in the case of David, Judas might well say: 'Let us fall into the hand of the Lord, for his mercy is great; but let me not fall into the hand of man' (2 Sam 24.14).

There is a text which is often cited to indicate God's will that all men should be saved: 'First of all, then, I urge that supplications, prayers, intercessions, and thanksgivings be made for all men ... This is good, and it is acceptable in the sight of God our Saviour, who desires all men to be saved and to come to the knowledge of the truth' (1 Tim 2.1,3-4). However, in the context, it appears that 'to be saved' is the equivalent of 'to come to the knowledge of the truth'; already in the Pastoral Epistles the latter term commonly means 'to accept the Christian faith' (1 Tim 4.31; 2 Tim 2.25; Tit 1.1). Thus it would not appear that the text bears directly on the final salvation of all men. One might argue that, if God wants men to come to the Christian faith, it is only because he wants to save them finally. Of course, this text, like most such texts in the New Testament, is not thinking of salvation outside the bounds of the Christian Church. Further theological reasoning is necessary if we are to extend such texts beyond the scope of the original writer.

In general, the hope of universal salvation discussed above seems to depend, not so much on any particular passage of Scripture, as on the very idea of God as revealed in the Bible (See J.A.T. Robinson, *In the End God*, London, 1968, pp. 110-118). God *is* love, according to 1 Jn 4.8; he is at the same time the almighty God: what God seriously wills he brings about in fact. While he respects the freedom of men, it is difficult to see how he is finally limited by it. Man, as he appears in history, has connatural deficiencies; socially and personally he is open to forces which he has to overcome to reach his fulfilment, forces which correspond to the Pauline *hamartia*. His defective and faltering steps along the way often appear as transgressions, inevitable but responsible concessions to the harmful forces which surround him. In the Pauline presentation of the Law, of justification, of grace, God can use the very transgressions of the believer to lead him to salvation. Allowing for the mysterious ways in which this loving God can communicate with the individual man (whether he is aware of the Christian revelation or not), have we any right to limit God's saving action to those alone who profess the Christian faith and are baptized? Ought we not extend this salvation to all men whom God, by the very fact of creating them, destined for final union with himself?

Admittedly, in the preceding section, we have been urging one part of the total biblical doctrine on the destiny of man. Any conclusions even suggested are provisional, since the whole question of judgment still has to be treated. It is an assumption demanded by Christian faith that the revelation of the New Testament provides a unity of doctrine. After expounding the New Testament doctrine on judgment, it will be our task to bring this theme into relationship with the preceding discussion on salvation.

Judgment

When we come to the New Testament teaching on judgment, it would be interesting to establish critically the authentic sayings of Jesus on this subject. It is a commonplace of New Testament scholarship that not every saying attributed to Jesus in the four gospels can be taken as actual words historically spoken by him. The peculiar literary form of the gospels, in which the words of Jesus were developed and modified to suit the needs of the later Church, warns us against an over simple interpretation (See *The Dogmatic Constitution on Divine Revelation* of Vatican II, ch.V, "The New Testament"). The early Christians, who believed in the presence of the risen Lord in the Church and in his word spoken through the inspired prophets in the Christian community, did not always distinguish clearly between the words of Jesus spoken historically and handed on through the tradition of the Church and those words uttered by him as Lord of the Church through the charismatic utterances of his prophets.

Seeing that there are such differences of opinion about the *method* by which we can rediscover the historical words of Jesus and consequently about the results of such investigation, it seems better simply to take the words ascribed to Jesus in the gospels and to discuss their meaning without endeavouring to distinguish between authentic sayings, extensions and modifications of such sayings, and finally sayings which do not correspond to any historical words of Jesus at all. All such words come to us with the warrant of inspiration and so are theologically and religiously normative for all Christian believers.

Mark

Let us start with the most primitive of the gospels, that of Mark. It may come as a surprise to note that there is little in this gospel which indicates a final judgment on man which would mean a perpetual rejection by God.

In Mark 9.43-48 we read:

> And if your hand causes you to sin, cut it off; it is better for you to enter into life maimed than with two hands to go to hell, to the unquenchable fire. And if your foot causes you to sin, cut it off. It is better for you to enter life maimed than with two feet to be thrown into hell.

> And if your eye causes you to sin, pluck it out; it is
> better for you to enter the kingdom of God with one
> eye than with two eyes to be thrown into hell, where
> the worm does not die and the fire is not quenched.

Commentators are agreed that we should not read back into
this passage the later teaching of the Church on the eternal
torment of hell. Jesus is using the accepted ideas of his time:
he does not question them or positively affirm them. What he
does express is a severe warning.

Here certainly two prospects are placed in front of men: 'to
enter into life', 'to enter into the kingdom of heaven', and 'to
go to hell', 'to the unquenchable fire', 'to be thrown into hell'.
We have already discussed the background of the term, hell,
geenna. Our text uses a citation from Is 66.24 to build up the
picture, but it is important to see this verse in its original
setting. First we have a magnificent picture of universal salvation:

> For as the new heavens and the new earth
>   which I will make
> shall remain before me, says the Lord;
>   so shall your descendants and your name remain.
> From new moon to new moon,
>   and from sabbath to sabbath,
> all flesh shall come to worship before me,
>   says the Lord (66.22-23).

Another writer felt that justice had not been done to the
enemies of God and so he added the following gruesome
description of their fate:

> And they shall go forth and look at the dead bodies of
> the men that have rebelled against me; for their worm
> shall not die, their fire shall not be quenched, and they
> shall be an abhorrence to all flesh.

Unfortunately this sombre verse remains the last word of the
great book of Isaiah. Jewish synagogue tradition felt the incon-
gruity of this end and always repeated the preceding message
of hope when the last section was read. Here, then, we have
summed up in one passage the problem we are seeking to

solve: universal salvation and judgment of the 'wicked'. Which is the last word to be spoken? But even in its own terms Is 66.24 deals with 'the dead bodies' of the wicked; it cannot be used to establish the later doctrine of an eternal hell.

Thus, it would be quite out of place to argue from a word such as 'unquenchable' in the Markan text that the final punishment of unrepentant sinners is literally everlasting. The term is simply taken from Is 66.24 and should not be pressed beyond its imaginative setting. Interpreters of former times who insisted on the literal meaning of the text might, with equal logic, have argued for the existence of immortal worms! The message which does come through, with force and clarity, is that the Christian must be prepared to sacrifice any possession, even the most precious, for the sake of eternal life.

Another passage from Mark which merits attention is 3.28-30. The context tells of the accusation of 'the scribes of Jerusalem' that Jesus was possessed by Beelzebub and that 'by the power of demons he cast out demons'. It is to such an attitude of wilful blindness that Jesus refers: 'Truly I say to you, all sins will be forgiven the sons of men, and whatever blasphemies they utter; but whoever blasphemes against the Holy Spirit never has forgiveness, but is guilty of an eternal sin — for they said, "He has an unclean spirit." ' This saying has a parallel in Mt 12.31-32 and Lk 12.10 (and therefore in their hypothetical source Q). Commentators are divided in their views about which is the more primitive version.

At first sight one might conclude that this passage is a verdict of damnation on the scribes mentioned in the passage. Yet, however details of the text are understood, this severe interpretation presents a considerable problem. It is hardly in keeping with the Christian understanding of God to hold that a group of men can be so categorically cut off from the possibility of future repentance and so consigned to hell, as it were, before their time. It is much more likely that we have here an emphatic and hyperbolic warning on the extreme evil of this attitude and of its possible consequences.

When this text is read more closely, it becomes evident that Jesus is not stating unequivocally that the scribes were actually guilty of 'an eternal sin'. But they are warned against an extreme hardness of heart which would shut out God's grace from their lives. The warning in Matthew (12.32) is even more emphatic: 'But whoever speaks against the Holy Spirit will not be forgiven, either in this age or in the age to come.' Are we to conclude that some sins will be forgiven in the age to come, that there is a particular sin which will, in fact, last forever? A statement like this is not to be taken as a theological thesis. Certainly final impenitence, by definition, cannot be forgiven. But one can still ask, from the background of what we have already seen of God's saving love, if in fact any human being will evade this love. Man by his sinfulness tends to the final inhumanity of absolute and irreversible alienation from God, but the fidelity of God remains forever. Here, as in the case of other texts, we must avoid the pitfall of piecemeal exegesis and try to listen to what the total gospel is saying.

In the longer ending of Mark's gospel (16.16) there is the statement: 'He who believes and is baptized will be saved; but he who does not believe will be condemned.' There is no doubt that salvation and condemnation here refer to the eschatological situation. Here, as so often in the New Testament, while the main force of the text must stand, the passage clamours for interpretation when applied concretely to human life. Even if the writer thought simply that all who materially hear the Christian gospel will be lost if they do not become Christians, further reflection of the Church has made it clear that, to merit condemnation, the rejection of the Christian gospel must be a responsible act of rebellion towards God. Certainly in our time we are aware how difficult it may be to present the gospel message adequately to the non-believer. However, here, as in the case of the text just discussed, we get the impression that, if there be such men who wilfully and totally resist the grace of God in rejecting the gospel, then for them eschatological judgment is the necessary consequence. But again one may ask whether any man so resists God's grace, so gives his heart to evil, that a completely negative sign sums up the value of his life.

Luke

The main contribution which the gospel of Luke has to offer on the subject of judgment and hell is the parable of the Rich Man and Lazarus (16.19-31).

While the religious message of the text is to be accepted with all reverence and faith, it must not be forgotten that it is presented in the form of a parable. It is the essence of a parable that a single lesson emerges presented in the context of common life and accepted beliefs. Now the point of the parable is primarily the reversal of fortunes in the life to come: the beggar Lazarus ends up 'in Abraham's bosom', while the rich man is tormented in flames. Nothing is said expressly of the moral attitudes of either, but Lazarus, no doubt, is the poor man who puts his hope in the Lord, while the rich man is indifferent to the needs of the beggar at his gate.

This moral lesson can be understood in the story. An Egyptian folk tale which probably lies behind our parable ends with the words: 'He who has been good on earth will be blessed in the kingdom of the dead; and he who has been evil on earth will suffer in the kingdom of the dead' (See J. Jeremias, *Rediscovering the Parables*, New York, 1966, p.145). The story was popular in Jewish circles and needed no further moral explanation. The second part of the parable, vv. 24-31, is an example of the doctrine that 'faith comes by hearing', not by spectacular signs.

Thus it would be a mistake to see in this passage principally a revelation about the situation of the dead. Jesus takes a story well known to his contemporaries and sets it in the context of his preaching of the kingdom of God. Hence it is difficult to see in this text any normative doctrine about the existence of hell. Hence we do not need to treat of the problem which so exercised earlier commentators: if those condemned to hell are perpetually and totally wicked, how is it that the rich man was charitable enough to think of his brothers on earth?

Matthew

It is in the gospel of Matthew above all that we find frequent references to judgment and hell:

> Whoever says, 'You fool!' shall be liable to the fire of hell (5.22).
> I tell you, many will come from the east and west and sit at table with Abraham, Isaac, and Jacob in the kingdom of heaven, while the sons of the kingdom will be thrown into the outer darkness; there men will weep and gnash their teeth (8.11-12).
> And do not fear those who kill the body and cannot kill the soul; rather fear him who can destroy both soul and body in hell (10.28; cf. Lk 12.5).
> The Son of man will send his angels, and they will gather out of his kingdom all causes of sin and all evil-doers, and throw them into the furnace of fire; there men will weep and gnash their teeth (13.41-42).

Similar references to hell are to be found in 13.49-50; 22.13; 23.15,33; cf. 11.22-23.

However the most solemn presentation of final judgment is that found in Mt 25.31-46. There is some discussion among commentators as to how 'all the nations' of verse 32 is to be taken. Does this refer to all mankind or simply to the Gentiles? It is much more likely that the phrase takes in all men. After all, the command of the risen Lord to make disciples of 'all nations' (28.19; cf. 24.9,14) certainly refers to all men; in addition, the place of this passage which comes as a climax of the eschatological section of the gospel, invites us to understand it as a picture of universal judgment: the whole of mankind will stand before the Son of man. Their final destiny is seen to depend on how they have treated the least of Christ's brethren.

One can also ask, who are these brethren of Christ? Are they simply Christian believers, or are they to be taken universally as any human being in need? In the setting of the gospel, it is possible that these brethren are to be understood as Christians, but in the original meaning of the text the term should be understood generally. Thus the passage is a sort of parallel to the Lucan story of the Good Samaritan (10.25-37).

But, apart from some details of interpretation, the text seems to present a clear picture. All men (or some of them) will hear the final verdict of the Son of man, and this verdict will be either 'Come, O blessed of my Father' or 'Depart from me, you cursed, into the eternal fire.' And the verdict will be executed in fact: 'And they will go into eternal punishment, and the righteous into eternal life' (v. 46). Here, surely, it might be argued, we have a clear and unequivocal statement on the existence of hell and on the way of life, human indifference to a brother's need, which leads to this utter and definitive human tragedy.

Some readers may feel, at this point, that it is completely unreasonable to hesitate, to engage in further subtleties of interpretation. Yet we are dealing with an ancient document, with a culture and literary form far removed from those we know. The obvious interpretation is not always the correct one. Some of us may remember the sound and fury which once accompanied the discussion of the beginning of Genesis: Was the world actually made in six days? It would seem wise to hesitate and reflect further when we are dealing with such an important topic, which deeply affects the religious life of Christians, who today are finding it increasingly difficult to give more than lip service to the strict doctrine of hell.

In the next chapter we shall discuss the general problem of the interpretation of eschatological statements. By way of anticipation, we may say that we are far from having in this text a sort of photographic anticipation of the final judgment, with the good and the bad lined up on the right and the left to be drafted off automatically to bliss or to misery. Secondly, the exact literary parallel in the passage between good and bad, their sentence and their destiny, calls for drastic interpretation. Jesus is not part Saviour and part Executioner. Unfortunately it seems easier to depict fear and utter misery than joy; one may well ask if the Christ of Michelangelo's famous painting in the Sistine Chapel does justice to the Jesus of the gospels. We run the incalculable risk of distortion when we try to translate the eschatological mystery of Matthew into the clear lines of a renaissance painting.

In fact, Jesus is Saviour only, not Executioner. There is no doubt about his welcome to the just and their entry into

39

eternal life. But, despite Michangelo's picture, there is, in the event, no parallel in his words to the wicked, no parallel in the fate depicted for them. As we have seen in other texts, we are not dealing with a scholastic theological thesis, but with an image. Nor is the problem clarified by the repetition of the term *aionios*, '*eternal* punishment', '*eternal* life'.

What we have in the text is fundamentally a blessing and a warning. Those who are indifferent to the needs of Jesus' brothers are revealed as truly wicked: they are caught in the grip of sin, and sin, of itself, being absolutely incompatible with the holiness of God, leads to final and complete alienation from him. But it is not affirmed that any human being, given the grace and mercy of God, ever arrives at this desperate situation. Even if we take the terms of the text itself, can it be affirmed that, in the life of any human being, there is absolutely no kindness or compassion for others? Rather the reader of the text is forced to reflect on himself. Where does he stand? If he is honest, he will admit that he belongs to both groups. Often, in areas where he least suspects it, he is indifferent to the needs of the poor. Even in the Church and by churchmen the poor can be held captive and go unpitied: 'They bind heavy burdens hard to bear, and lay them on men's shoulders; but they themselves will not move them with their finger' (Mt 23.4). Let the Christian reader, then, confess his sin and commit himself and all men who share his sin to the mercy of his Lord and Saviour.

Paul

Among the earlier writings of Paul there is a passage which vividly recalls the judgment scene of Mt 25.31-46:

> This is evidence of the righteous judgment of God, that you may be worthy of the kingdom of God, for which you are suffering — since indeed God deems it just to repay with affliction those who afflict you, and to grant rest with us to you who are afflicted, when the Lord Jesus is revealed from heaven with his mighty angels in flaming fire, inflicting vengeance upon those who do not know God and upon those who do not obey the gospel of our Lord Jesus. They shall suffer the punishment of

eternal destruction and exclusion from the presence of the Lord and from the glory of his might (2 Thess 1.5-9).

The background of this passage is that of the Day of the Lord as presented in the Old Testament particularly by the prophet Isaiah (Cf. Is 2.10,19,21; 66.15). Those who do not 'know' God, that is, those who do not acknowledge him by faith, those who do not 'obey the gospel', will be excluded 'from the presence of the Lord' and so will be condemned to 'the punishment of eternal destruction'. Here, it could be argued, Paul is thinking of the annihilation of the sinners; but the mere use of the term *olethros* does not give ground for this view. This can equally mean 'ruin', and it is this meaning which seems to be required by the context.

Commentators are not agreed as to whether those who do not know God are a separate group from those who do not obey the gospel. In any case, whatever may be said of the detailed points of exegesis, the thought of Paul (or of the interpolator, if 5.6-10 is to be taken as a later addition) calls for interpretation. In the first place, this attitude of unbelief condemned in the text must be a responsible one: it will not do simply to relegate to this category any self-styled unbeliever. Particularly in our day, an unbeliever may be a sincere person who rejects belief in God as proposed to him. In this attitude he may, at least in part, be quite justified. Secondly, when this unbelief is responsible and culpable, it puts a man on the way of sin, and sin, of itself, brings a man to final condemnation. In the context, Paul is thinking particularly of those Jews who were persecuting the Thessalonian Christians. Yet, here too, it would be pressing the text altogether too far to think of such people as in some way rigorously destined to eternal damnation. To the degree that men reject with full responsibility the gospel message and show that rejection by persecuting the Christian Church they come under God's condemnation. But the text cannot be adduced to show that any individual will actually incur final damnation.

That all men, including Christians, will have to face final

judgment is a recurring theme in Paul's letters: 'For we must all appear before the judgment seat of Christ, so that each one may receive good or evil, according to what he has done in the body' (2 Cor 5.10). This text seems to imply that each man will be judged immediately after death. While the Christian longs to reach his perfect fulfilment, to enjoy the new life of bodily resurrection (5.1-2) which Paul expected would come to him in his life-time, he knows that even if he were to die before the parousia he will be 'at home with the Lord', and he knows also that the verdict of the coming judgment may not be entirely favourable, since a man must give an account of his evil deeds as well as of his good deeds. The optimistic tone of the earlier section (5.1-9) scarcely permits the thought of absolute damnation in 5.10. What form this possible condemnation might take is not expressed.

In the threatening first part of Romans, where Paul builds up the picture of human sin, we read:

But by your hard and impenitent heart you are storing up wrath for yourself on the day of wrath when God's righteous judgment will be revealed. For he will render to every man according to his works: to those who by patience in well-doing seek for glory and honour and immortality, he will give eternal life; but for those who are factious and do not obey the truth, but obey wickedness, there will be wrath and fury (Rom 2.5-8).

Similarly, in Phil 3.19, Paul can say of those who, while professing to be Christians, are unfaithful to their calling: 'Their end is destruction!' The general principles lying behind this judgment are expressed in Gal 6.7-9: 'Do not be deceived: God is not mocked, for whatever a man sows, that he will also reap. For he who sows to his own flesh will from the flesh reap corruption; but he who sows to the Spirit will from the Spirit reap eternal life.' Here the contrast is between 'corruption' and 'eternal life'. Later in Rom 8.13 Paul sums the matter up: 'For if you live according to the flesh, you will die, but if by the Spirit you put to death the deeds of the body, you will live.' Here life is simply contrasted with death (cf. Rom 6.23a).

More expressly in 1 Cor 6.9-10 Paul describes the sort of

life which, even for a Christian, will incur condemnation: 'Do you not know the unrighteous will not inherit the kingdom of God? Do not be deceived; neither the immoral, nor idolaters, nor adulterers, nor homosexuals, nor thieves, nor the greedy, nor drunkards, nor revilers, nor robbers will inherit the kingdom of God.' Thus, according to Paul, those who do not 'know God', who 'do not obey the truth but obey wickedness', who 'live according to the flesh', who practise immorality prevalent in the pagan world, all these will face eschatological condemnation.

Since it is above all Paul who gives a more elaborate theology of salvation and of sin, it might be worthwhile here to outline some points which are central to our discussion:

1) Paul supposes that men are responsible and free beings: they are free to accept the gospel message or not, and, having received it, they are free to live according to it, 'according to the Spirit', or to live contrary to it, 'according to the flesh'.

2) On the other hand, justification is a free gift of God, which man cannot of himself deserve by any good work or by any free decision (Rom 3.21-26).

3) It can be presumed, therefore, that there is no contradiction between man's responsibility and God's bestowal of the Spirit through justification.

4) Once justified, a man can be secure in hope that God's grace will triumph in him (Rom 5.1-11). 'Hope does not disappoint us, because God's love has been poured into our hearts through the Holy Spirit which has been given to us' (Rom 5.3).

5) God's attitude to the sinner is that of 'wrath': in this way the complete incompatibility between the holiness of God and sin is indicated.

6) Despite the fact that God is a saving God, and despite the fact that those who are finally saved are saved through his grace (and not merely through the correct exercise of free will), Paul certainly does present a picture of final judgment and condemnation of those who reject the gospel or who remain obdurate in wickedness.

7) One can still ask whether Paul, in presenting this judgment, is, strictly speaking, referring to an actual future event or whether he is warning his readers about the destiny which would await men if finally they did not come under the grace of God.

8) One can further ask (given above all a more modern understanding of human psychology) whether the apparent rejection of the gospel, or various forms of apparently sinful behaviour among professed Christians need necessarily involve a radical and responsible rejection of God. How a man reacts to God's grace in the depths of his heart is God's secret.

9) If, then, any professed Christian, despite his awareness of his own sinfulness and of the possibility of further sin, can firmly hope in his own final salvation, it may be asked by what right he excludes this hope, whatever mysterious form it may take, from the heart of any other human being.

10) One can at least ask whether the picture presented by Paul of the final condemnation of sinners is to be interpreted as the judgment passed by God on any man *in so far* as he is a sinner. The *final* nature of this judgment indicates the *absolute* incompatibility between God and sin. At the same time, Christ died for all men; human sin is seen as explicable only as a stage on the way towards the triumph of God's grace:

> For as by one man's disobedience many were made sinners, so by one man's obedience many will be made righteous. Law came in to increase the trespass, but where sin increased, grace abounded all the more, so that, as sin reigned in death, grace also might reign through righteousness to eternal life through Jesus Christ our Lord (Rom 5.19-21).

Thus Paul can sum up: 'For God has consigned all men to disobedience, that he may have mercy on all' (Rom 11.32).

Hebrews

The author of the Epistle to the Hebrews speaks in the severest terms of the judgment awaiting those who commit the sin of apostasy from the Christian faith:

44

> For it is impossible to restore again to repentance those who have once been enlightened, who have tasted the heavenly gift, and who have become partakers of the Holy Spirit, and have tasted the goodness of the word of God and the powers of the age to come, if they then commit apostasy, since they crucify the Son of God on their own account and hold him up to contempt. For land which has drunk the rain that often falls upon it and brings forth vegetation useful for those who have cultivated it, receives a blessing from God. But if it bears thorns and thistles, it is worthless and near to being cursed; its end is to be burned (6.4-8).

There is a similar condemnation of apostasy in 10.26-27,31: 'For if we sin deliberately after receiving the knowledge of the truth, there no longer remains a sacrifice for sins, but a fearful prospect of judgment, and a fury of fire which will consume the adversaries . . . It is a fearful thing to fall into the hands of the living God.'

Taking these texts at their face value, one might draw the conclusion that the apostate from the Christian faith, like the man who blasphemes against the Holy Spirit (cf. Mk 3.29,par.), was already damned and that the only possible fate awaiting him was eternal burning. From the second passage above it would follow that, while the apostate remains in culpable obduracy, he has cut himself off from his one source of salvation and so is destined only to judgment and condemnation. Note that the whole situation is put hypothetically: 'If we sin deliberately. . .' The difficult word in the first passage is the 'impossible' (*adunaton*) of 6.4.

As a matter of fact, this apparently very severe text is open to quite another meaning. Most modern translations suppose that the word 'impossible' must be linked with the conversion to repentance of the sinner. A careful re-reading of the Greek text (which was originally free of punctuation) supports an interpretation which connects 'impossible' with the actual repetition of the one saving sacrifice of Christ:

> As for those who have once been enlightened, who have tasted the heavenly gift, who have been partakers of the Holy Spirit, and who yet have fallen away, for these it is

impossible to effect a renewal by crucifying again for one's self and putting to public shame the Son of Man and so providing a means of repentance.

No, the apostates must return and find salvation in the one saving death of Jesus. This cannot be repeated for their sake. Thus the text anticipates the thought of 10.26-27, 'there no longer remains a sacrifice for sins', a severe warning, but certainly not an absolute condemnation. The reader who desires a fuller discussion of this text may read the article (in Spanish) of P. Proulx - L. Alonso Schoekel, 'Heb 6.4-6: *eis metanoian anastaurountes*', *Biblica* 56 (1975), p. 193-199.

John

There is not a great deal to add to the New Testament picture of hell from the Johannine writings. The Fourth Gospel is primarily concerned with the judgment passed here and now on the man who does not believe the good news. But this form of 'realised eschatology' does not exclude the traditional picture of a final eschatological judgment. Whether one ascribes to the historical Jesus a form of 'realised eschatology', as maintained by Dodd, or a form of 'final eschatology', a view popularised by Schweitzer, one thing is clear: in the Fourth Gospel, as it now stands, there is to be found, along with the 'realised eschatology', a genuine tradition of 'final eschatology', and the hypothesis of Bultmann of an 'ecclesiastical redactor', who touched up the Johannine presentation of 'realised eschatology' in the interests of orthodoxy, does not seem soundly based.

The condition for 'entering the kingdom of God' in Jn 3.5 is to be 'born of water and the Holy Spirit'. Given the context of the passage, 'entering the kingdom of God' would seem to be the equivalent of 'having eternal life' (cf. 3.16), which, in Johannine terminology, refers to present possession rather than to a fulfilment to come. In any case, only a wooden and uninspired interpretation would simply relegate to present or final condemnation all those who, for any reason, have not received Christian baptism. There is a remarkable parallel between this text: 'Truly, truly, I say to you, unless one is born of water and the Spirit, he cannot enter the kingdom of God' (3.5) and: 'Truly, truly, I say to you, unless you eat the flesh of the Son of man and drank his blood, you have no life in you' (6.53). Both texts are concerned with the Church, entry into it and life within its fold. It would be unwarranted to extend them beyond this ecclesial context to an affirmation of the absolute necessity of baptism and the Eucharist for all men, whatever their condition.

More expressly, belief in Jesus is presented as a means necessary for eternal life: 'He who believes in the Son has eternal life; he who does not obey the Son shall not see life, but the wrath of God rests upon him' (3.36; cf. 3.18; 15.6).

As in the case of other passages, this text clamours for interpretation. No doubt the author of the gospel was thinking simply of the proclamation of the Christian message and of its acceptance or rejection by the hearer. Modern man is much more aware of the problem of communication and much less ready to speak confidently of what goes on in a human heart. The fundamental meaning of the text stands: all men must come to Jesus with faith in some way if they are to find eternal life. The Fourth Gospel itself insists that: 'God so loved the world that he gave his only Son, that whoever believes in him should not perish but have eternal life' (3.16). If God's love for the world is real, then all men are invited, in some mysterious way, to believe in Jesus and so have eternal life. Particularly in modern times when even to men of good will the Church itself is seen as an ambiguous sign, texts like this cannot be strictly limited to a matter of church affiliation. We cannot affirm that any man has persisted or will persist in a responsible and obdurate refusal to come, in his own personal and mysterious way, to Jesus.

Yet there is one passage in the Fourth Gospel, more general in scope, which re-echoes the doctrine of judgment we have already seen in the synoptics: 'Do not marvel at this, for the hour is coming when all who are in the tombs will hear his voice and come forth, those who have done good to the resurrection of life, and those who have done evil to the resurrection of judgment' (5.28). We have already discussed the judgment scene of Mt 25.31-46; nothing need be added here, except to comment briefly on the new idea in Jn 5.28 of the 'resurrection to judgment'. In general, in the New Testament, the resurrection of the body is seen as a sharing in the life of the risen Jesus, 'who will change our lowly body to be like his glorious body, by the power which enables him to subject all things to himself' (Phil 3.21). Thus resurrection is not just a continuing in existence of the human person: it is a mystery of new and eternal life. At first sight, resurrection to death seems a contradiction in terms. Are we to think of some sort of miraculous resurrection produced sheerly by the vindictive justice of God so that the total human person may suffer eternally?

The apparent parallel, resurrection to life and resurrection to judgment, must be interpreted along the same lines as the corresponding parallel in Mt 25.46, that of eternal life and eternal punishment. Here the writer takes up the idea of the resurrection of the wicked found in Dan 12.2. Evil separates man from God and, of itself, tends to bring him to utter ruin. It matters little how this final ruin is depicted: it remains mysterious and hypothetical. It is not actually stated that, for any man, the power and love of God will be finally thwarted.

In 1 Jn 5.16-17 we have the problem of the 'mortal sin': 'If any one sees his brother committing what is not a mortal sin, he will ask and God will give him life for those whose sin is not mortal. There is a sin which is mortal; I do not say that one is to pray for that. All wrongdoing is sin, but there is sin which is not mortal.' One might here question the translation 'mortal sin' for the phrase *hamartia pros thanaton*. This sin is rather one which tends to death, which will end up in death if not checked.

Commentators associate this sin with that of Heb 10.26-31, where the fearful situation of the apostate is described. In the absence of further information we may take it that apostasy is the 'sin unto death' which the writer is alluding to. Note that John does not say that this sin cannot be forgiven, nor does he forbid prayers to be offered for such a sinner. But he does refrain from prescribing prayers for such a person. From the

48

context one gathers that there is question of public, liturgical prayer (cf. Jas 5.14-15). One should not be surprised at the limitations of such prayer. For centuries it was the custom in the Church's liturgy to pray only for those 'of the household of the faith'. Hence this text throws no light on the problem of final judgment.

Revelation

Associated in Christian tradition with the Johannine writings is the Book of Revelation. This association is still maintained by a considerable number of modern commentators. The literary form of this book leads one to expect a grand and picturesque vision of eschatological judgment.

In 2.11; 20.6,14; 21.8 the writer speaks of a 'second death'. This phrase echoes the ideas of Dan 12.2 and Jn 5.29. A parallel is to be found in Philo's account of the punishment of Cain: 'What is this punishment? That he should live forever in a state of dying and so to speak suffer a death which is deathless and unending.' *(De praem. et poen.*, 12. 70. For evidence of this expression in Jewish tradition especially in the Targums, see Strack-Billerbeck, V.3, pp. 830-831.) This second death is associated in 21.8 with 'the lake that burns with fire and brimstone', the punishment of 'the cowardly, the faithless', and the polluted, murderers, fornicators, sorcerers, idolaters, and all liars.

The first group mentioned is to be understood of disloyal Christians: the 'cowardly' are those who give up the faith in time of persecution (cf. Mk 9.35-37); the 'faithless', in this case, are probably not only the pagans (cf. 1 Cor 6.6; 7.12-15; 10.27; 14.22-25; 2 Cor 6.14-15), but also Christians who have turned from Christ. The second group represents the various vices prevalent among the pagans in New Testament times.

More explicit is the punishment threatened to the worshippers of Caesar:

And another angel, a third, followed saying with a loud voice, 'If anyone worships the beast and its image, and receives a mark on his forehead or on his hand, he also shall drink the wine of God's wrath, poured unmixed into the cup of his anger, and he shall be tormented with fire and brimstone in the presence of the holy angels and in the presence of the Lamb. And the smoke of their torment goes up for ever and ever; and they have no rest, day or night, these worshippers of the beast and its image, and whoever receives the mark of its name.' (14.9-11).

While the fate of all worshippers of Caesar is here depicted, the passage is presented above all as a warning to Christians who might be tempted to take this course. This is a reply to a proclamation of the beast in chapter 13, 'that no one can buy or sell unless he has the mark, that is the name of the beast or the number of its name' (13.17). A much worse fate than this awaits those who prefer Caesar to Christ. Just as Christians who were faithful to Christ were liable to suffer publicly as a spectacle to their fellow men, so the renegade Christian will suffer in the sight of the angels and of the Lamb. The punishment of Sodom and Gomorrah is recalled: 'And lo, the smoke of the land went up like the smoke of a furnace' (Gen 19.28b), and also the fate of Edom:

And the streams of Edom shall be turned into pitch,
      and her soul into brimstone;
      her land shall become burning pitch.
Night and day it shall not be quenched;
      its smoke shall go up for ever (Is 34.9-10a).

Here, as in the case of Matthew, ch.25, the author is concerned to give a serious warning to Christians in danger of being untrue to Christ. One can ask to what degree he wishes to predict and describe the future. The fact that he takes up the stereotyped phrases from the Old Testament, there applied to Sodom and Edom, surely is an indication that he is not offering a factual description of the future. It will be only after we have had the opportunity to study more deeply the interpretation of eschatological warnings that we will be able to appreciate what the author is really saying about the future.

After the binding of the devil and the reign of Christ for a thousand years (20.2-3,4), and the final eschatological battle against Gog and Magog (20.7-9), 'The devil who had deceived them was thrown into the lake of fire and brimstone where the beast and the false prophet were, and they will be tormented day and night for ever and ever' (20.10).

Then comes the final judgment which heralds in the new Jerusalem:

> And I saw the dead, great and small, standing before the throne, and books were opened. Also another book was opened, which is the book of life. And the dead were judged by what was written in the books, by what they had done. And the sea gave up the dead in it, and Death and Hades gave up the dead in them, and all were judged by what they had done. Then Death and Hades were thrown into the lake of fire; and if any one's name was not found written in the book of life, he was thrown into the lake of fire (20.12-15).

In this picture of the final judgment, it is God himself who is the judge: those whose names are not found written in the book of life are thrown into the lake of fire. Curiously enough, the personified Death and Hades both suffer the same fate. One might have thought that, with the overcoming of Death and Hades, that all human beings would be released from their grip; yet those whose names are not written in the book of life are eternally in the thrall of death. One might also ask whether it could not be inferred from the parallel states of the wicked and of Death and Hades that, just as the punishment of the last two is a mythological presentation of their annihilation, so too this might be the ultimate end of the wicked. While in apocalyptic writing we are not to look for full consistency, we are at least reminded of the fact that we are dealing with images, and thus we are forewarned that any interpretation which insists that we have here a wooden, factual prediction of the future is misguided from the beginning. Such images, based on past experience and literary references, can do no more than mirror, in a way proper to themselves, the yet mysterious future.

Thus the book of Revelation gives us the most emphatic and detailed picture of hell. It is supposed in 20.12-13 that there will be a resurrection for condemnation. In 14.11, it is stated that the torment of the worshippers of Caesar will last forever, but these terms are taken from the Old Testament account of the punishment of Edom (Is 34.10). Given the apocalyptic imagery of the whole passage of Isaiah ch. 34, in which 'all the host of heaven shall rot away, and the skies roll up like a scroll', one may doubt whether the prophet envisaged anything like a strict eternity of punishment for Edom. And so one may ask further whether the application of this imagery in the passage of Revelation is meant to convey anything more than an impressive warning, with no dogmatic statement about a strictly eternal punishment.

The Catholic Epistles

In the letter of James we read: 'Their desire when it has conceived gives birth to sin; and sin when it is full-grown brings forth death' (1.15). Death here is not merely physical death: it includes also spiritual death. In the context, this death is evidently eternal. It has the same meaning as the Pauline *thanatos:* 'For the wages of sin is death' (Rom 6.12). In the context here the contrast with 'eternal life' (6.22) makes it clear that Paul is thinking of eternal death. But the text of James and its counterpart in Romans do not necessarily imply that any particular man will find himself in the situation of eternal death. While such death is the natural consequence of sin, it is precisely the role of Jesus Christ to intervene as the Saviour of men and to prevent this outcome.

According to James, the tongue is 'set on fire by hell (*geena*)' (3.6). This is a picturesque way of saying that evils perpetrated by the human tongue originate from the devil, whose abode is the gehenna of fire (cf. Mt 25.1). Nothing further can be derived from this text on man's future fate.

The diatribe against the rich in 5.1-6 includes a threat of future retribution: 'Your gold and silver have rusted, and their rust will be evidence against you and will eat your flesh like fire. You have laid up treasure for the last days' (5.3). It is possible to link *pur* with *ethesaurisate* and so translate the verse with the Jerusalem Bible: "It was a burning fire that you stored up as your treasure for the last days." If we take the first interpretation, supported by the majority of translators (e.g., RSV, NEB), editions (e.g., that of K. Aland, M. Black, B.M. Metzger and A. Wikgren, and that of A. Merk), and commentators (e.g., H. Windisch — H. Preisker, J. Schneider, J.B. Mayor), then the term 'fire' is used metaphorically. In fact, the whole text is highly metaphorical: the rust of silver and gold will consume the flesh of the rich. No doubt the writer is thinking of the punishment of the next life, since this is contrasted, in verse 5, with this life: 'You have lived on the earth in luxury and in pleasure.' Again, it is not clear whether 5:3b is to be taken ironically: 'You have laid up treasure for the last days.' The NEB version does not interpret the text in this way: 'You have piled up wealth in an age that is near its close.' Others, e.g., Mayor, suggest that the passage is to be interpreted ironically: 'You heap up treasures, but the time for enjoying such treasures has come to an end: it is now only a treasure of wrath in the day of wrath.'

It is clear that James shares the view of other New Testament writers that those who are wicked in this life, who yielding to their own lust commit sin (1.15), who, in particular, are faithless and selfish in the use of this world's goods (5.3), will run the risk of punishment in the next life. All will have to give an account to God: 'There is one lawgiver and judge, he who is able to save and destroy' (4.12).

While the whole tone of 1 Peter is strongly eschatological (see E.G. Selwyn, 'Eschatology in 1 Peter', *The Background of the New Testament and its Eschatology. Studies in Honour of C.H. Dodd*, Cambridge, 1956, pp. 394-401), there is in it little reference to future judgment. In 4.5 there is mention of the judgment facing the Gentiles who mock the Christian believer: 'But they will give account to him who is ready to judge the living and the dead' (cf. Mt 12.36. For a full treatment of 1 Pet 4.5-6, see W.J. Dalton, *Christ's Proclamation to the Spirits*, Rome, 1965, pp. 263-277). This theme is taken up again in 4.17-18: 'For the time has come for judgment to begin with the household of God; and if it begins with us, what will be the end of those who do not obey the gospel of God? And if the righteous man is scarcely saved, where will the impious and the sinner appear?' For the believing Christian judgment in the form of persecution ends in salvation. For those who 'do not obey the gospel of God' judgment will involve something far worse. This warning is put in the form of a question: there is no actual description of the judgment of the unbeliever (cf. 2 Thes 1.8-9; Rev 6.15-17). What the writer has left vague should be left vague: he has nothing to say more specifically about the punishment of the wicked. Nor does he provide us with any criterion as to who, really and responsibly, is to be regarded as one who rejects the gospel.

The epistle of Jude, concerned as it is with the dangers of false belief, emphasises the theme of judgment. The writer draws on examples of God's punishment of sinners in the past to attack the violent language and vicious behaviour of false Christians. While the angels who sinned with women, according to the Jewish tradition founded on Gen 6.1-2, were punished in 'eternal chains in the nether world until the judgment of the great day', the sinful citizens of Sodom and Gomorrah 'serve as an example by undergoing a punishment of eternal fire' (v. 6-7). Here the writer is recalling elements of Jewish tradition (cf. 4 Macc 12.12; 1 Enoch 67) according to which a fiery place of punishment was situated under the Dead Sea. The evil Christians opposed by Jude are threatened with similar punishment in the words of 1 Enoch 1.9: 'Behold the Lord came with his holy myriads, to execute judgment on all and to convict the ungodly of all their deeds of ungodliness.'

The faithful Christians are exhorted to try to help those in such mortal danger: 'Save some by snatching them out of the fire.' The 'fire' of this text is the eschatological fire of hell. It presents no problem to the writer that already in verse 13, in his diatribe against the false Christians, he calls them 'wandering stars for whom the nether gloom of darkness has been reserved forever'. Here the darkness associated with *sheol* in Jewish tradition passes over to *gehenna* (1 Enoch 45.3; cf. 2 Enoch 10.2).

Hence the writer of Jude accepts without question the picture of future judgment for sinners prevalent in Jewish tradition and applies it to the faithless Christians of his day.

54

In 2 Peter, which in its chapter 2 is heavily in debt to Jude, it is said of the 'false prophets' that 'from of old their condemnation has not been idle, and their destruction has not been asleep' (2.3; cf. Jude 3). The Lord knows how 'to keep the unrighteous under punishment until the day of judgment' (2.9b). For such men, 'it would have been better for them never to have known the way of righteousness than after knowing it to turn back from the holy commandment delivered to them' (2.21; cf. Heb 6.4-8). As in Jude 13, for the false teachers 'the nether gloom of darkness has been reserved' (2.17b). Thus they will share the lot of the wicked angels 'whom God cast into hell (*tartaros*) and committed to pits of nether gloom to be kept until the day of judgment' (2.4).

The writer does not develop the theme of hell fire, but presents a picture of the parousia in which the present world will be destroyed by fire: 'But by the same word the heavens and earth that now exist have been stored up for fire, being kept until the day of judgment and destruction of ungodly men' (3.7). Here the fire which will dissolve the universe is connected with the 'destruction' (*apoleia*) of the wicked. In itself the word 'destruction' could mean 'annihilation' or simply 'ruin'. In the context, the old universe will be destroyed: 'Then the heavens will pass away with a loud noise, and the elements will be dissolved with fire, and the earth and the works that are upon it will be burnt up' (3.10). Thus we might conclude that the wicked, who have been kept in 'nether gloom' up to this point, will also share in the annihilation of the old universe. Since they have given themselves to this world, one might suppose that they will share its fate. We must ask again whether the eternal fire of this text and of others in the New Testament is to be taken as strictly eternal. It is worth noting that, although in Jude 7-8 the 'chains' and 'fire' are called 'eternal', yet all these are to give way to a new situation at the 'judgment of the great day'. Similarly in 2 Peter 2.4, *tartaros* is a place of confinement *until* judgment. The 'extinction' (*katastrophe*) of Sodom and Gomorrah (2 Pet 2.6) is 'an example to those who were to be ungodly'. While *katastrophe*, like *apoleia*, can also mean 'ruin' (cf. 2 Tim 2.14), there can be no doubt that complete destruction is referred to in Peter 2.4.

It seems that in Jude and 2 Peter, while there is a hell envisaged for wicked angels and men (Jude 6-7,13; 2 Pet 2.4,6,9), and while this hell is called 'eternal' (Jude 6-7), yet this hell is a provisional abode for the wicked awaiting the last judgment. While Jude does not make any more explicit statement as to what will happen to the wicked on the day of judgment, 2 Peter (which does not mention the eternal fire of hell) makes much of the eschatological fire of judgment, which will destroy both the old world and all ungodly men. Note that in 2 Peter 2.12 the author speaks of the *future* destruction of the false teachers, by which they will share the fate of brute beasts, whereas the corresponding passage in Jude 10 refers to the sinners' present undoing.

It would seem then that, while Jude leaves open and undefined the actual issue of God's judgment of the wicked, 2 Peter at least tends to understand this judgment as their annihilation.

Summary Of New Testament Doctrine

At this point we shall try to sum up what we have seen of the two apparently conflicting themes in the New Testament, that of universal salvation and that of eternal damnation of the wicked. The first seems to be founded on the nature of God himself as he is shown with full evidence in the New Testament: God is love (1 Jn 4.8); he is the father who welcomes the return of the prodigal son (Lk 15.11-31); his Son is the good shepherd who goes after the lost sheep (Jn 10.11). When Jesus is lifted up, he will draw all men to himself (Jn 12.32); it is the work of this Son to reconcile all things to God (Col 1.20); in the end God will be everything to every one (1 Cor 15.28) and the last enemy to be destroyed will be death, both bodily and spiritual (1 Cor 15.26; cf. Rom 5.21).

The initiative in the whole work of salvation and the carrying through of this work, both come from God:

He destined us in love to be his sons through Jesus Christ, according to the purpose of his love (Eph 1.5).

> For by grace you have been saved through faith, and this is not your own doing, it is the gift of God — not because of works, lest any man should boast. For we are his workmanship, created in Christ Jesus for good works, which God prepared beforehand, so that we should work in them (Eph 2.8-10).

Thus, both faith and a life of good works are God's gifts. It is part of Christian dogmatic tradition that those who are finally saved are saved by God's grace, not by the correct use of free will (Dz 238-242, etc.).

If one asks how human sin fits in with this salvific plan of God, the answer can be given in the words of Paul: 'God has consigned all men to disobedience, that he might have mercy on all.' This disobedience is not merely the violation of the Jewish Law but all forms of law. Recalling the situation of the fall of the first human pair, Paul writes: 'I once was alive apart from the law, but when the commandment came, sin revived and I died; the very commandment which promised life proved to be death to me. For sin, finding opportunity in the commandment, deceived me and by it killed me' (Rom 7.9-11). In fact, in the religious development of man, it was necessary that sin should be revealed for what it is through transgression of the law. This experience, then, of what we would call now actual sin is caught up in the economy of salvation. Given the sinful situation of man, the law which provokes transgression becomes a means of revealing to man his dire need of God and of thus preparing his heart for the grace of God: 'Law came in, to increase the trespass; but where sin increased, grace abounded all the more' (Rom 5.20). 'For no human being will be justified in his sight by works of the law since through the law comes knowledge of sin' (Rom 3.20).

In the ideal order, once a man is justified, he is dead to sin and to the law: this is the meaning of Christian baptism (Rom 6.3-11). Yet Paul's constant exhortations to live a Christian moral life imply the possibility of sin even after conversion and baptism: 'Let not sin therefore reign in your mortal bodies to make you obey their passions' (Rom 6.12). It is only too clear that early Christian communities often found it difficult to make a clean break with their pagan past: 'Do you not know that the unrighteous will not inherit the kingdom of God? Do not be deceived: neither the immoral, nor idolaters, nor adulterers, nor homosexuals, nor theives, nor the greedy, nor drunkards, nor revilers, nor robbers will inherit the kingdom of God' (1 Cor 6.9-10). Paul allows for such a situation in Gal 6.1: 'Brother, if a man is overtaken in any trespass, you who are spiritual should restore him in a spirit of gentleness.' In this he was following the doctrine of Mt 18.15: 'If your brother sins [some manuscripts add: 'against you', but this is better omitted], go and tell him his fault, between you and him alone. If he listens to you, you have gained your brother.' This is in keeping with the final instructions of the Epistle of James: 'My brethren, if any among you wanders from the truth and someone brings him back, let him know that whoever brings back a sinner from the error of his way will save his soul from death and will cover a multitude of sins' (Jas 5.19-20). For such Christians who do not live up to the ideal of Christian life, who despite their baptism are still, to some degree, under the tyranny of sin, the general doctrine of Paul would still apply. Their yielding to temptation and their transgressions are a form of self-expression, an expression of a carnal self still, to some degree, under the dominion of sin. *Sarx*, 'flesh', in the language of the New Testament signifies the total man in so far as he is weak and deprived of the light and strength of the Holy Spirit. This revelation of their real state and of their need for grace should be for them a humble beginning of a new conversion and a new effort to dedicate themselves to the ideal Christian life.

Thus, both before and after conversion to Christianity, sin can be seen as an event which God can and does use to lead men to closer union with himself. In the history of the Church there is no dearth of examples to illustrate this divine economy by which saints evolve from notorious sinners. Note that in every such case the initiative is with God: to God is given the glory when a man is converted to the Christian faith, when a Christian returns, after a serious failure, to the ideal of

Christian life. Man cannot claim the glory under the pretext that, after all, he has freely chosen to receive the grace of God. This human self-reliance is seen by Paul as the great obstacle to Christian faith. This purely human wisdom, which expresses itself in 'boasting', must give way to the wisdom of God (1 Cor 1.18-31). The tradition of the Church has ratified this Pauline doctrine, seeing especially in final perseverance a special gift of God (Dz 1572).

It follows that, in the case of those who are to be finally saved, sin is permitted by God as a stage in man's progress to God. But while God positively predestines his elect, it is of Catholic faith that he does not, in similar fashion, positively predestine others to eternal damnation (Dz 1567).

With this background we should approach the texts in the New Testament which bear on the eternal damnation of the sinner. Such texts are numerous enough, but must be read in the total context of God's word, which reveals a God of salvation, not of damnation. Again they must be read as examples of prophetic warnings, not primarily as predictions of the future. The option of accepting the gospel message or of not accepting it, of living a Christian life or of not living a Christian life, is seen to be fraught with immense consequences. If a man obstinately perseveres in rejecting the gospel, if a Christian perseveres in a responsible and serious deviation from the Christian way of life, he is on the path to disaster. The inward dynamic of evil, if it follows its own course, will lead him to what the New Testament calls exclusion from the Kingdom of God, external darkness, eternal fire. But one can still ask: Has anybody followed, will anybody follow this path of evil to the bitter end? It is true that the human imagination in its literature has attempted to portray men who are utterly evil without the relief of any quality which might be called good. In fact, by a strange and not particularly admirable twist, the imagination is often more fascinated by evil than good. Human experience does not seem to bear out such a pessimistic view of mankind: I have yet to meet someone who seemed totally bad; I have yet to meet someone who would declare confidently that he has met another human being who is totally bad.

It is important to remember that damnation in the New Testament is always hypothetical: *if* a man continues along the path of evil, under the influence of evil ... Fortunately for man, in the actual context of his life, there is a Father who is concerned for him, who offers him his grace at every point, who belongs to him by a free covenant of love, who cannot hate what he has made, who is immanent to the core of his being because he is the creator, who is pledged to save his son if this is at all possible.

So we come to the final question: Can human sin, in fact, thwart the infinite and persevering love of God? Is it possible, in fact, for a man to be eternally damned? Is this possibility the only sincere conclusion to be drawn from the pages of the New Testament? Before we offer a final comment on such a conclusion, it will be necessary to consider more fully how we should interpret eschatological statements.

Chapter III

INTERPRETATION OF ESCHATOLOGICAL STATEMENTS

A valuable and penetrating approach to this question has been offered by Karl Rahner in his essay, 'The Hermeneutics of Eschatological Assertions' (*Theological Investigations*, Vol. 4, London, 1966, pp. 323-346. Cf. also H. Urs von Balthasar, 'Eschatology', ed. J. Feiner, J. Trutsch, F. Bockle, *Theology Today*, Vol. 1, Milwaukee, 1965, pp. 222-244). Rahner points out that this problem has hardly ever been dealt with expressly in Catholic theology (p. 323). Thus, while there is an urgent need for this problem to be faced, it is particularly difficult to handle, and conclusions must remain, to some degree, tentative.

One of the chief difficulties in this area is the persuasion 'that the eschata form a world like any other, so that a knowledge of them — in spite of its being determined, like other knowledge, by the object itself — presents no particular problems apart from those of the knowledge of theological realities in general' (Rahner, p. 324). It is not sufficient to take any particular eschatological assertion and to trim it, as it were, to suit modern ideas about the universe and of man. It is even less adequate to make an arbitrary selection of eschatological elements, keeping some and rejecting others. For example, why should we insist on retaining the material fire of hell while we treat darkness and worms as purely metaphorical? We must go further and investigate what such assertions, of their very nature, are capable of communicating, and what principles can be established to ensure a correct interpretation of such assertions. Rahner himself suggests that the correct method would be that of biblical theology: the principles involved should be suggested by the Scriptures themselves (pp. 324-325). He does not follow this path himself, but, in the investigation which follows, takes his stand upon basic dogmatic considerations.

In this difficult and hitherto little explored area, the

present writer does not pretend to offer any adequate biblical theology concerning eschatological statements. Rather he will attempt to treat along biblical lines some of the matter proposed in Rahner's pioneering essay.

The first question to be asked is whether eschatological assertions say anything at all about the future, or whether they bear totally and exclusively on man's present. This is not an idle question. While Catholic tradition has always understood such statements as referring to a real future (Rahner, p. 326), one could still perhaps argue that, since this question had not been raised explicitly in the past, this dogmatic tradition should be regarded as still open to interpretation and modification. In any case, outside Catholic circles, this question has been put expressly in modern times. Indeed, the beginnings of such an interpretation is seen to be present in the New Testament itself, in the eschatological approach of the Fourth Gospel. Thus 'eternal life' is for the believer not so much an experience of the future: it is a present reality (Jn 5.24). Conversely the man who rejects God's call will not have to wait for future judgment: his judgment takes place here and now (Jn 3.18-19). It is not our business here to discuss the elements of a future eschatology which appear in the Fourth Gospel. It cannot be doubted that the dominant trend is that of present fulfilment.

Among modern scholars, Bultmann especially has urged the need for interpreting the cosmological and transcendent elements in New Testament eschatology. The framework of such eschatology belongs to the past, a past which has no longer relevance for modern man. What is important for the man of today is his present religious experience. This present experience is the goal of history, and, in this way, it can be called eschatological. Thus Bultmann can end his work, *Presence of Eternity: History and Eschatology* (Edinburgh, 1957): 'But now we can say: *the meaning in history lies always in the present*, and when the present is conceived as the eschatological present by Christian faith the meaning in history is realised.'

The contribution of C.H. Dodd to the interpretation of

eschatology is well known. While not denying the coming to an end of human history, he insists that the point of New Testament eschatology is that, with the ministry of Jesus Christ, the kingdom of God has actually arrived. Successive generations, through the proclamation of the gospel, must face this fact and make their decision accordingly. Hence in no sense is the Kingdom realised through a historical progress, and it does not in any way evolve towards a culmination. The future has no real meaning because history has no real meaning. The emphasis is exclusively on the response of faith to the event of Jesus presented in the Christian proclamation here and now. Dodd's 'realised eschatology' is best exemplified in his *Parables of the Kingdom* (1st ed. London, 1935). In his later writings, including the fourth edition of the same work in 1948, he has maintained the same general position in face of fairly general criticism.

Neither of these views seems to do justice to the general biblical presentation of man, a communitarian being, rooted in a historical process, who lives not merely by faith but by hope. Thus, it would seem that Cullmann's theory of Salvation-history (*Heilsgeschichte*) is more faithful to the general trend of Old and New Testament writings — prescinding from the vexed question of the personal attitude of Jesus himself. For a good modern survey of this latter problem, one could consult N. Perrin, *The Kingdom of God in the Teaching of Jesus* (London, 1963). Whatever one may think of the details of their interpretation, the modern theological developments of Pannenberg and Moltmann (J. Moltmann, *Theology of Hope*, London, 1965; J.M. Robinson, J.B. Cobb, edd., *New Frontiers in Theology, Vol. 3, Theology as History*, New York, 1967) give due attention to the seriousness with which the Bible takes the condition of man as a being set in time and history.

Without developing at any length the historical nature of Old Testament religion, it is surely clear that the God of the covenant was a God of promise; he demanded of his people not only faith but hope, confidence in his fidelity. While the future destiny of the individual after death remained obscure, the community, whose existence was rooted in history, looked to God to fulfil his promises. The fulfilment of these promises remained mysterious. At each step along the way, God spoke to his people not merely by word but by event: no inspired word about the future was a simple photographic prediction: the future remained God's future. This pattern of mysterious fulfilment is exemplified, above all, in the final messianic climax. God, in his sovereign freedom, was to fulfil his word, but in a way which was quite personal to himself. Whether final fulfilment is conceived in history or beyond history, it is God's work and God's future, a future which transcends the thoughts and imaginings of any man, even those of his inspired prophets.

But, one might say, this Old Testament historical development, according to the writers of the New Testament, came to an end with Jesus of Nazareth: the coming of Jesus was seen as the fulfilment of the Old Testament promises of salvation. In a sense this is so. Whatever the teaching of Jesus on the subject, the early Church certainly thought that all history was to come to a close in the near future.

Thus, the Last Times, in the hope of the Christian community, were to endure only for a brief period. But even this period was not removed from human history. The disciples were not simply to sit around waiting in utter passivity for the moment of the parousia. They were to preach the gospel to the world (Mt 28.19-20; Mk 16.15-16; Lk 24.46-47). There was a mission to all men and a progress of that mission. This progress and development is seen above all in the theology of Luke. Salvation is brought to the world in the stages of a great journey: that of Jesus to Jerusalem, and, after the establishment of the Church at Jerusalem, the movement of Paul, the envoy of Jesus to the Gentiles, outwards to the pagan nations and finally to Rome itself, the capital of the great pagan world. Luke is at pains to put these happenings in the framework of universal history (2.1-2; 3.1). While Luke does not lose the perspective of final fulfilment, it is equally true that he sees the Church moving towards this hour through real human history.

Thus, though the Christian finds himself in the Last Times, he is not removed from history: he is a man of hope like his predecessors in Israel, only the foundation of his hope is immensely greater: it is the person of Jesus Christ, with whom he is united by faith and baptism, and who, as risen Lord, beckons him on to the full sharing of his resurrection. And this hope is not merely individual. Man as an embodied spirit is a member of a community; by his baptism he belongs to the Church, a fellowship which is sealed and strengthened by the Eucharist. And so it is the whole pilgrim Church which looks forward to the final coming of the Lord and whose inmost prayer is *'Marana tha'* (1 Cor 16.22).

Basic to the Christian's hope in a personal salvation to come is the event of Jesus' resurrection. If faith in the resurrection of Jesus merely means that the work of liberation begun by Jesus continues among his followers, then, while the circle of Jesus' disciples and, for that matter, the human race may have a corporate future, the individual Christian believer may well abandon hope in a personal future beyond this earthly life. The philosophical doctrine of the immortality of the soul is far too fragile to found a real life of hope. But if, on the contrary, Jesus is truly risen from the dead, if he really lives now as Lord, then he personally has won the victory over death. More than this, Jesus died and rose *for us:* 'but in fact Christ has been raised from the dead, the first fruits of those who have fallen asleep' (1 Cor 15.20). Paul's great treatment of the resurrection of Christ and the resurrection of Christians in 1 Cor 15 is one of the fundamental texts of Christian faith. Despite some difficulties in interpretation, one thing is eminently clear: for Paul the resurrection of the man Jesus is a real event in the experience of Jesus himself and real in the tremendous consequences of all those who share his life.

When Paul wrote of the resurrection he was thinking primarily of Jesus and the Christian believer; but in the re-flection of the Church it is seen that all men, whether they have heard the Christian gospel or not, are called to salvation through Christ. Thus Paul's perspective can be legitimately developed to reveal an apocalyptic scene even more splendid than that of 1 Cor 15. In this all men, of every time, race and religion, who share, each in his own mysterious way, the faith of the Christian believer, will share also his moment of fulfilment when he joins his Lord in glory.

Thus, in the doctrine of the resurrection, the two streams of eschatology meet: the corporate future of man moving as a pilgrim through history and the personal future of the individual. The individual, in his personal hope, gives depth to the corporate hope of the Church and the world. In fact, it is one single hope which respects the nature of man, embodied spirit set in the midst of the material universe.

It should be clear then that the eschatological statements of the New Testament, set in the context of a community in history, must refer to a real future. Any interpretation which fails to recognize or do full justice to this cannot fail to distort the message of the New Testament.

Given the fact that these statements do refer to the future, we may now ask, *how* do they refer to the future. In particular, are we to take them as factual predictions of the future? Note that the precise problem is not whether God can communicate a factual knowledge of the future (Rahner, pp. 326-327). The question rather is whether, in the eschatological assertions of the New Testament, he actually does so.

A simple examination of New Testament texts reveals that such statements about the future cannot be taken literally, since, if taken in this way, they contradict one another. In fact, we may well doubt whether any prophetic prediction in the Bible is to be taken in a sheerly factual way. For example, the glorious return and the establishment of the new Israel foretold by second Isaiah were never factually fulfilled. Israel had to learn through its long history that prophecies made in the name of God were fulfilled in God's own way: he was not bound to the letter of the prophet's word. Rather it was the future event, produced by the Lord of history, which revealed the full meaning of the prophet's word.

And so, when we come to the New Testament, we are forewarned not to expect a purely factual fulfilment of prophetic statements about the future, especially when these statements refer expressly to the new mysterious order of eschatological fulfilment. Thus it would be very unwise to insist that Jesus at a certain day and hour and moment will appear visibly in the clouds of heaven, that a throne will be set up somewhere, that a trumpet will be heard, that the graves will be opened and the dead will be seen arising, that the good will be led to his right hand and the wicked to his left, and that he will be bound by the juridical formulas of the twenty-fifth chapter of Matthew. And if we insist on the reality of the fire which will torment the wicked, why do we not insist on immortal worms? And, on the other hand, why do we not insist on a messianic meal where specific food and drink will be shared? And are we bound to make a choice between 2 Peter 3.7, where the complete destruction of the universe by fire is depicted, and the account of Romans 8.19-23, where the whole of creation is seen to be groaning awaiting, not its destruction, but its redemption and fulfilment?

It should be clear that such eschatological assertions are not simply predictions and that it is an arbitrary procedure to choose some factual elements and to exclude others without establishing a firm basis for doing so.

We may take it that in such statements the future remains God's mysterious future: it is not possessed by man in some form of intellectual anticipation. Man as he moves through history constantly looks back on his past, interprets and knows the present in the light of that past. Inevitably as a being of hope he looks to the future: he has to use the categories of the past and the present to speak of the future. Yet, unless he possesses some miraculous anticipation of the future, which may not be supposed, he must leave the future open to God's mysterious ways. For him the knowledge of the future is not a simple transportation forward in time, where, from a new vantage point, he has an experience of observing reality similar to his experience of his present existence. For a Christian such knowledge is based above all on the present revelation communicated to man as to who God is and what he has done in his saving work through Jesus Christ.

This understanding of the sovereign freedom of God, by

which he refused to be enclosed within the bounds of cyclic time, by which he personally disposes of men and events, by which he escapes the categories even of his prophets, such an understanding is an inheritance which passed from the Old Testament to the New (cf. G. von Rad, *Theology of the Old Testament*, Vol. 2, New York, 1965, pp. 99-118).

But the final question remains. Given that eschatological assertions do refer to the future, given also that they are not simple factual predictions of the future, what then do they actually say of the future?

They say that the God who redeemed us through the death and resurrection of his Son, whom we meet by faith in the Christian community, is a faithful God, that he keeps his promises in his own personal way, that he takes man seriously as an embodied spirit, a free responsible being set within his community in the flow of history.

Hence, positively, eschatological statements are messages of present grace and salvation which open out into God's mysterious fulfilment. Thus we read in 1 Jn 3.2: 'Beloved, we are God's children now; it does not yet appear what we shall be, but we know that when he appears we shall be like him, for we shall see him as he is.' While it is true that we must take with equal seriousness eschatological statements of condemnation, it is most important to realize that assertions about salvation and those about judgment are not to be put on the same level. The God revealed in the New Testament, and, for that matter in the Old, is a saving God, not a damning God. Here the picture of final judgment in chapter 25 of St. Matthew's gospel can be very misleading unless correctly interpreted. One can easily forget the inadequate analogy between Jesus Christ and a human judge. A human judge is appointed by public authority to administer the law. He decides in each case whether the law has been observed or violated. He stands under the law and, as judge, he plays a role quite different from that of a saviour. In a sense, once the evidence has been given, he merely acts as a traffic policeman, directing some to salvation, others to damnation. Jesus, on the other hand, is the good shepherd who gives his life for his sheep, who goes after the lost sheep and rejoices when it is found. If he does pass judgment on men, it is because, despite all his love and suffering and prolonged invitation to faith and a life of faith, for some inscrutable reason such men refuse and reject him, and, in a real sense, condemn themselves. In this way Jesus really judges no one: it is man who rejects the light and life he offers: 'For God sent the Son into the world, not to judge the world, but that the world might be saved through him. He who believes in him is not condemned; he who does not believe is condemned already, because he has not believed in the name of the only Son of God' (Jn 1.17-18). However, then, the predestination of the just is to be understood, it can never be such as to require a sort of parallel predestination of the wicked to damnation.

What, then, do eschatological assertions about damnation mean? One thing is certain: they are not bits of esoteric information about the eternal fate of some individuals. Everything said in the New Testament is, in one way or another, said for us men and for our salvation. Hence such statements are primarily warnings addressed to men whom God wishes to save. God respects man's freedom and requires from him willing love and service. He warns him of the immense and mysterious consequence of obstinate refusal to return his love, and, in the human language of Jesus and of the New Testament writers, this mysterious and awful situation is described in the conventional terms available: fire, darkness, worms, gnashing of teeth. One could imagine that, in a different culture and with a different literary background, quite different terms might have been used.

We still have to face the most difficult problem of all. Once we admit that God is a God of love and at the same time the Lord of men and history, can we admit, at the same time, the possibility that one of his human creatures could be finally and absolutely damned? Bishop Robinson, in his work, *In the End God* (London, 1968), makes out an eloquent case for universal salvation. And from the texts we have already discussed above this would seem to be a genuine biblical theme.

Note that it is not necessary to insist on the actual loss of one or of a number of human beings to upset the universalist position. It is enough to admit that it is a real possibility that some human beings should fail to reach salvation. If this is possible, then the actual damnation of some would not be a denial of the true nature of the Christian God.

But here we have need to pause. God is too mysterious and the possibilities of his relationships with men too incomprehensible to be summed up in some metaphysical statement. Hence the term 'real possibility' is ambiguous. We would do better to limit ourselves to what could be called a *practical* possibility and to leave the question of *absolute* possibility to the mystery of God himself. In human terms, I may be practically certain, for example, that I am loved by a friend, even though there does remain the absolute possibility that I am deceived. Despite this possibility I may rightly build my life on the conviction that I am truly loved. So here the question rather is: From what I know of God and his ways with men, may I be practically sure that he will actually save all? May I act on this conviction in thinking and talking of the gospel of Jesus Christ?

Robinson speaks of sinners who choose eternal death: 'As they choose it and as long as they choose it, it is something that must present itself to them (or be made to present itself to them) as a choice which is final and irreversible' (p. 130). This is what eternal punishment means: a situation which, apart from the grace of God, is irreparable. However, in actual fact, given the total context of human life which includes God's offer of pardon and grace, such a situation is not merely reversible, but, according to Robinson, either in this life or in the next, it will certainly be actually reversed (p. 133).

According to Robinson, this transference from a myth depicting hell to an actual state of human beings after death makes the mistake of objectivizing this mythical picture 'as a description of the final condition of the universe as it is in God . . . What is of eternal moment becomes what is of everlasting duration' (p. 132). Thus it is supposed that conversion to God from sin would be possible after death. This would not seem to be in keeping with Catholic tradition. Yet this avenue might well be explored. There is an equally Catholic acceptance of purgatory, for which no really satisfactory explanation has been given. What happens to the man who is fundamentally just, but who in many areas of life is self-centred and sinful, when he comes at death before the all-holy God? Terms such as passive purification do not help a great deal. The man himself must co-operate with God in a free, radical re-orientation of his life. If this is not to be called conversion, it is at least, under the grace of God, some form of contrite renewal. Can we really be so confident about what God can do or not do in his mysterious future?

Even if we were to admit that a man totally bad at the moment of his death could have no part in eternal life, but must remain fixed in his evil, we can still ask once more: can any human being be totally bad? After all, God loves him and all are called by God to love him. God does not separate his love for him as a thing, which he keeps in being, from his love for him as a person. When I meet a so-called sinner, I am not called to love him hypothetically; even when he is at the moment of death, I love him as a brother without condition. If I have prayed for and suffered with the dying person, it seems outrageous that I should be told: 'He didn't make it; you are forbidden to love him any more; he is in hell.'

Nor is it much consolation to know that he is not 'in hell' in the traditional sense, but that he has simply dropped out of existence. From the time of Arnobius, efforts have been made to mitigate the apparent cruelty of the doctrine of eternal punishment by a theory of conditional immortality or resurrection. Until recently this view was popular in certain Protestant circles, but unknown to Roman Catholics. But now it is emerging as an acceptable alternative among Catholic writers. It has been proposed by T. McDermott (*New Blackfriars* 48 [1967], pp. 186-197) and by M. Simpson (*The Theology of Death and Eternal Life*, Cork, 1971). This solution is logical enough within its own terms of reference. After all, eternal life is a gift of God. The idea of resurrection for damnation has always seemed a strange concept; and the concept of the natural immortality of the soul supposes a

71

philosophical view of human nature which has its own problems.

Yet surely Simpson points to the real difficulty when he emphasizes the solidarity of all men, particularly their solidarity in sin: 'How can he accept a hope in which the "wicked" — who are wicked perhaps precisely through his failure — are relegated to a world of eternal punishment and doom?' (p. 9; cf. p. 93).

On the other hand, this writer affirms the 'logical possibility' of a totally selfish man simply falling out of existence, or, if this solution is not accepted, of some form of temporal existence in which separation from God continues forever. He concludes: 'In either case the reality of hell is still affirmed as a real possibility of man's eternal destiny' (p. 80). It is difficult indeed to square this with the author's other emphasis on the solidarity of all men: 'I share the eternal destiny of others, they share in mine' (p. 93). In the hypothesis of the damnation of a totally selfish person, we can take it for granted that he succumbed to the sin of the world, the evil context of life which other human beings helped to create.

A similar attempt to solve the problem of an eternal hell was made by T. and G. Sartory (*In der Holle brennt kein Feuer*, Munchen, 1968). According to these authors, the doctrine of an eternal hell strictly does not belong to Christian revelation: it is part of the cultural and religious inheritance which Jesus and the New Testament writers received from the past (pp. 214-218). One can still ask what is the fate of a human being so devoid of love that he totally denies his humanity. Having denied his humanity he has renounced all claim on eternal life (pp. 234-235). But the authors do not seem to face the problem of human solidarity. While they accept the inextricable mixture of good and evil which is found in every man and while they refuse to divide the world into the 'good' and the 'bad' (pp. 230-235), they accept with apparent equanimity the hypothesis of a totally evil human being. Obviously such a person would have no eternal place with God, and, in fact, he would have no place anywhere. But one must still ask: can he so easily drop out of the lives of those who prayed for him, who hoped for him, who loved him?

So we come back to the fundamental problem: if any of my brothers ends up in an eternal hell, can I be truly saved? And we can push further than Simpson our co-responsibility in sin. I can affirm that every sin of mine adds to the contagion of the world's sin. This goes far beyond bad example or personal influence. We are all partly responsible for the future sins of other men. Even when we emphasise the fact that men sin freely, our responsibility remains. And allowing to the full for the mysterious nature of our life in God's future, we are faced with a brutal enigma indeed if in that life we have to miss (but not to mourn!) the lost brother we helped to damn, whether it be a damnation of punishment or nothingness.

Chapter IV

THE DOCTRINE OF HELL TODAY

So far we have considered the Bible and the interpretation of the Bible in discussing the topic of hell. This consideration remains fundamental. Later Church tradition, no matter how authoritatively proposed, supposes the exegesis and interpretation current at the time when it is expressed. In a fuller work, one could look at this tradition more in detail; but the story, at least within the Catholic Church itself, is a fairly simple one. By and large, with a few notable exceptions such as Origen, the Catholic Church has presented a united front: eternal punishment for obdurate sinners, which, until quite recent times, included a literal understanding of everlasting fire. In the last decade or so, there has been quite a dramatic change. Few scholars would propose a literal understanding of hell. Few would maintain that it is of divine revelation that in fact any human beings are or shall be condemned to hell. And there have been developments, such as those noted above, which would understand hell as simple annihilation. However, it would still be generally held that the possibility of hell (understood as eternal separation from God or annihilation) must be retained.

Before leaving the Catholic scene, we might note that the condemnation of Origen in the Synod of Constantinople in 543 (Dz 411) had a considerable effect in closing the discussion about the eternity of hell. However it is important to understand where precisely the error in Origen's system lay. It can be urged that it was the denial of human freedom which led to the condemnation of his doctrine of *apokatastasis*, the final restoration in which all men and spirits would be saved. In other words, if one could combine full respect for human (and angelic) freedom with an acceptance of universal salvation, then such a view would not come under this condemnation. This opinion has been proposed by W. Thompson (in *The Ecumenist*, 10 [1972], pp. 33-37) and is worthy of consideration.

Among Protestant groups, there has long been an uneasiness about the eternity of hell. One has only to read the fascinating work of D.P. Walker, *The Decline of Hell* (London, 1964) to see how these discussions ranged during the seventeenth century. With the following centuries the more optimistic view of final human destiny grew ever stronger. One of the outstanding achievements of Protestant theology was Schleiermacher's *The Christian Year*. This great thinker espoused the cause of universal salvation and insisted that the New Testament was open to such an interpretation. In the continuing debate, the dispute which arose in England between F.W. Farrer and E.B. Pusey is worthy of note. The former published his *Eternal Hope: Five Sermons Preached in Westminster Abbey, November and December, 1877*. Despite his pleas to the contrary, the book was understood as an indirect defence of universal salvation, and, as such, was attacked by Pusey in his work, *What is of Faith as to Everlasting Punishment* (3rd ed., Oxford, 1881). In this he insisted, above all, on the strict understanding of 'eternal' as applied to the punishment of hell (pp. 38-106).

But a friend of Pusey, E.H. Plumptre, came out once more in defence of universalism in his book, *The Spirits in Prison* (London, 1898), basing his argument on the obscure text of 1 Pet 3.19. The exegetical basis of this view has been accepted, in more recent times, by Bo Reicke in his *The Disobedient Spirits and Christian Baptism* (Copenhagen, 1946). For a totally different interpretation one might consult the monograph of W.J. Dalton, *Christ's Proclamation to the Spirits* (Rome, 1965). The atmosphere at the end of the nineteenth century is well summed up in a passage from Tennyson's *In Memoriam* which ends:

> I stretch lame hands of faith, and grope,
>   And gather dust and chaff, and call
>   To what I feel is Lord of all,
> And faintly trust the larger hope.

This 'larger hope' has, since this time, been consistently proposed by representative Protestant Theologians. One such writer was Isaak August Dorner, whose two volume work, *System der christlichen Glaubenslehre* (Berlin, 1880), was widely read and, in its English translation, deeply affected the theological thought of the United States. Dorner allows for conversion and moral progress in the next life and thus can hold out hope for universal salvation.

Karl Barth, while never opting expressly for universalism, would seem logically to suppose such a view in his treatment of reconciliation (*Church Dogmatics, Vol. 4*, trans. G.W. Bromley, Edinburgh, 1956, pp. 19-128). For Barth the measure of a Christian's hope for himself is that of his hope for others (p. 119). Emil Brunner criticized Barth severely for his apparent universalism (*The Christian Doctrine of God, Dogmatics, Vol. 1*, trans. O. Wyon, London, 1949, p. 349), but he himself seems to arrive at a similar view when he states his own position (*Eternal Hope*, trans. H. Knight, Philadelphia, 1954; *The Christian Doctrine of the Church, Faith and the Consummation, Vol. 3*, trans. D. Cairns and T.H.L. Parker, Philadelphia, 1962, pp. 415-424). Brunner admits that there is a logical contradiction between the biblical doctrine of salvation and judgment, but he insists that the problem must be taken outside the sphere of objective knowledge: the man of faith is summoned by God to a personal confrontation. Only in hearing the word of judgment can he understand the grace of the gospel. So Brunner can say: 'We have confidence that we shall be brought safely through the judgment by the grace of God' (p. 421). It is ironical that he, in turn, comes under fire from the conservative Protestant scholar, H. Buis, for ending up in the universalist camp (*The Doctrine of Eternal Punishment*, Philadelphia, 1957, p. 107).

Other modern Protestant theologians of note, in one way or another, seem to arrive at similar conclusions. R. Niebuhr touches on the problem of hell in his treatment of "The New Testament Idea of the End" (*The Nature and Destiny of Man, Vol. 2, Human Destiny*, New York, 1941, pp. 287-298). Having rejected the literal interpretation of eschatological statements in favour of one which is symbolic, he concludes: 'There is no solution of the final problem short of divine mercy and the "forgiveness of sins" (p. 292).

Paul Tillich will not accept either a facile *apokatastasis* or the division of mankind into those finally saved or damned (*Systematic Theology, Vol. 3, Life and the Spirit, History and the Kingdom of God*, Chicago, 1963, p. 407). He insists on the social solidarity of all men (p. 409) but insists equally on preserving the sharp contradiction between eternal life and eternal death (p. 418). He himself presents a 'more adequate answer' based on his concept of the relationship between eternity and time: 'Time and change are present in the depth of Eternal Life, but they are contained within the unity of the Divine Life' (p. 418). Despite the obscurity of Tillich's philosophical background, it seems evident that he rejects the traditional Christian teaching, even in its most mitigated form, on heaven and hell. Every man, for him, is finally purified of the evil associated with earthy existence; whatever good there is in him is saved and transformed into eternal life.

We have touched on the work of J.A.T. Robinson in the preceding chapter. He sums up very aptly the theological developments of earlier writers. His work, *In the End God* (London, 1968), was a new version of an earlier book and, following on the lively controversy provoked by the same author's *Honest to God*, immediately became popular. Robinson has shown great sensitivity in reflecting the attitudes, trends and feelings of many modern Christians. He maintains that, despite the firm attitude of traditional Christianity on individual eschatology, the New Testament itself 'never dogmatizes to the extent of saying that after death there is no further chance' (p. 44). He goes on to insist that every eschatological statement is really a statement about God, a God of mercy and love, whose final word cannot be destruction (p. 49).

When facing the apparent contradiction between universal salvation and the division separating the lost from the saved, he rejects the Calvinistic view of double predestination; he does not accept the opinion which would permit the damnation of some while hoping for the salvation of all, nor can he abide what he calls the traditional solution, which declares that 'God will be all in all despite the damnation or destruction of many of his creatures' (p. 113).

Like Brunner, he gives up any solution to the problem of salvation and hell in the objective order. In the subjective order of the 'I - Thou' relationship of meeting, both extremes are, to his mind, respected. He presents no facile picture of easy salvation. As far as man is concerned, if he chooses death, his choice is final and irreversible (p. 130). On the other hand, the believer is sure that God will not let the matter rest there. He will finally win all for himself.

In a final parable (p. 133) he pictures the road leading to destruction crowded with sinners. Somewhere along this road each one meets a figure bowed beneath the weight of the cross, and 'no man in the end can bear that encounter forever'. The sinner freely but inevitably yields to God's love.

Conclusions

This writer belongs to the Roman Catholic Church and wishes to remain within it. It is within the context of this church that he thinks and writes. The following conclusions are presented with this context firmly in mind. It is a question of interpreting one's faith, not of departing from it.

One must insist on the word *interpretation*. A literal interpretation, as opposed to a symbolic one, is still an interpretation. In the effort to understand ancient religious documents, which belong to a culture very different from ours, a literal interpretation has no prior claim nor can it be regarded as 'safer'. It is simply a question of trying to find out, in the light of all the evidence, what is true. So the charitable reader is invited to join in this search for truth, to credit the writer with the desire to serve both his church and the truth, even when all or some of these conclusions may seem objectionable.

1. There has been a great change recently in the Catholic understanding of hell. From the time of Augustine, through the Middle Ages to modern times, the literal interpretation of

hell prevailed. Even the slight doubt of Petavius about the corporeal nature of hell-fire had to be sternly rebuked. One has only to read the classic work of L. Billot, *Quaestiones de novissimis* (7th ed., Rome, 1938) to note the scholastic subtlety with which an extremely literalist view is defended. Even modern science is invoked by A. Michel to explain the peculiar nature of corporeal, everlasting fire, in his article, 'Feu de l'enfer' (*Dictionnaire de Theologie Catholique*, 5.2196-2246). As late as 1950 we find roughly the same teaching in the volume, *L'enfer*, published by a group of French Catholic scholars. The teaching of St Thomas Aquinas is re-affirmed: the fire of hell is material fire; this fire is eternal.

But now through the slow process of biblical education, certain conclusions seem quite firm: the eschatological statements of the New Testament are seen to demand a symbolic interpretation. There is no question of material fire. As we have seen, there are Catholic scholars who propose that the eternal punishment of the damned might well be simply their annihilation. It is accepted that it is not a matter of faith that a single human being will ever end up in hell. We are a long way from the "massa damnata" of Augustine. In all this process, not merely have the biblical texts been more correctly interpreted, but the many official statements of the teaching church, which supposed at the time of their composition a literalist understanding of these texts, have been reinterpreted. One thing is certain. It will not do to cite phrases from church councils as though they had a value quite independent of the biblical texts they suppose. Thus in the first Ecumenical Council of Lyons we are required to believe that the damned 'are forever tortured in the fires of everlasting gehenna' (Dz 839). Whatever the fathers of the council thought, their words today are misleading, even erroneous, if they are not interpreted symbolically.

2. This development of the church's understanding of hell provides a deeper insight into the Christian revelation, not a departure from it. Are further developments required? It is still stated by Catholic writers that we are required by faith to accept the possibility of damnation (understood as continued

existence or annihilation) for any individual human being. To put it in another way, I or any other human being could end up in unrepented moral evil, for which hell is the only fitting consequence. The following remarks are offered by way of comment on this view.

i) The solidarity of all men (with the material creation) in both sin and salvation would seem to be undeniable biblical teaching.

ii) Despite the apparent parallel between eternal life and eternal punishment (see Mt 25.46, etc.), there is in fact no real parallel. The God of the New Testament is not half-saving, half-punishing: he is the God of salvation.

iii) If God is a saving God and if he can save all men, then he *will* save all men.

iv) The crucial point is whether God can save all men, given that men are free to choose good or evil. Man's freedom must be respected. It was the denial of this freedom which seems to lie behind the condemnation of Origen's theory of *apokatastasis*. Yet to this writer it seems by no means evident that God cannot do both, that is, save all men and also respect their freedom.

3. What then are we to make of the constant biblical references to judgment, to the final condemnation of the wicked?

i) It is suggested that these references should not be interpreted separately, but seen in the light of God's salvation. Man is sinful: he tends to evil: of himself, without the grace of God, he moves to self-destruction, to final alienation from God. *In so far* as he shuts himself up in his own selfishness and resists God's grace, he comes under God's judgment. But given the persevering love of God, this judgment becomes a purifying experience, by which this sinner-son enters into eternal life.

ii) But what of the man who wrecks his own life completely, who dies completely without love? No doubt novelists with a macabre turn of mind have tried to invent such people; but one can well doubt whether this is true to life. Other human beings are bound to love the so-called sinner; no man is so low that he can rightly be excluded from human respect and concern. If a man is at all lovable, he must have at least the beginnings of love somewhere in his heart. And, as we have seen, this so-called sinner in the family of man is part of my flesh and blood, without whom the rest of the race cannot be fully saved.

iii) The extreme black and white eschatological picture which appears in the sayings of Jesus and in the New Testament generally denotes a deep concern for ultimate human values rather than a prediction of the future. As we have seen, one could understand the eternal fire of gehenna as part of the apocalyptical furniture accepted without question into the New Testament. As such, it does not belong to the Christian revelation.

4. But the question can be asked: Will the strong moral fibre of genuine Christian life be weakened once the austere teaching of eternal fire for the damned is removed? My reflections on the result of fear in Christian life lead me to the opposite conclusions. So many Christians are fear-ridden, whether they stick to the literal understanding of hell or not. The calls of the New Testament to confidence, joy and exultation leave them cold. Their God is more the personification of duty than the Father. The good news of God's grace in Jesus never seems to get through the barrier of their anxiety. It can hardly be said that the traditional doctrine of hell has helped to establish a fundamental attitude of faith and trust. One might well question the 'morality' which finds its basis in fear.

5. Finally, can we offer some general conclusion at the end of our long discussion about salvation and judgment? We must stand by human freedom. We must also stand by the traditional Church doctrine that, if a man ends his life totally alienated from God, he cannot live with God in his eternity. But given the splendid fidelity of God and his power to save, we may well ask whether such a man has ever existed or will ever exist. It would be difficult to deny the abstract possibility of such a case: even for the holiest of men it would be difficult to deny the abstract possibility of a lapse into total sinfulness

at the end of life. But God has revealed himself as a faithful saving God; he has put into our hearts a persevering love for our fellow men and an intense feeling of our abiding solidarity. Christian faith itself calls on us to extend our hope beyond ourselves to all other men.

Our conclusion then is a theological opinion, not a dogmatic assertion, that we may have real hope that all men will finally be saved. By hope I do not mean merely an abstract hope in God's love and fidelity: I mean hope in his actual and effective love for me and all others. And this salvation remains from beginning to end an absolute grace bestowed with sovereign freedom by God. It is not for us to dictate to God how he should act; he seems to have given us enough evidence of his ways with men to enable us to draw our own conclusions.

In his letter to the Romans, Paul delved deep into the mystery of human sin, the sins of the pagans and the astonishing sin by which Israel rejected its Messiah — he did not underrate sin. Let us end with his words:

> For God has consigned all men to disobedience, that he may have mercy on all. O the depth of the riches and wisdom and knowledge of God! How unsearchable are his judgments and how inscrutable are his ways! (Rom 11.32-33).

SELECT BIBLIOGRAPHY
of works available in English

General treatments of eschatology are not listed unless they deal with the precise topic of this book.

BALTHASAR URS VON H., "Eschatology", *Theology Today I* (ed. J. Feiner et alii), Milwaukee, 1965, pp. 222-244.

BARTH K., *Church Dogmatics IV*, Edinburgh, 1956, pp. 79-128.

BARTH K., *The Humanity of God*, London, 1961, esp. pp. 61-62.

BRUNNER E., *Eternal Hope*, Philadelphia, 1954.

BUIS H., *The Doctrine of Eternal Punishment*, Philadelphia, 1957.

CROUZEL H., "Apocatastasis", *Sacramentum Mundi I*, London, 1968, pp. 51-52.

DODD C. H., *The Parables of the Kingdom* (4th ed.), London, 1948.

GUY H. A., *The New Testament Doctrine of the 'Last Things'*, London, 1948.

McDERMOTT T., "Hell", *New Blackfriars*, 48(1967)186-197.

MOLTMANN J., *The Theology of Hope*, London, 1965.

MOORE A. L., *The Parousia in the New Testament*, Leiden, 1966.

MOULE C. F. D., "The Theology of Forgiveness", *From Faith to Faith: Studies of Suffering and Loneliness* (ed. N. Hutton), London, 1971, pp. 61-72.

NIEBUHR R., "The New Testament Idea of the End", *The Nature and Destiny of Man II, Human Destiny*, New York, 1941, pp. 287-298.

RAHNER K., "The Hermeneutics of Eschatological Assertions", *Theological Investigations IV*, London, 1966, pp. 322-354.

RAHNER K., "Eschatology", *Sacramentum Mundi II*, London, 1968, pp. 243-246.

ROBINSON J. A. T., *In the End God*, London, 1968.

SIMPSON M., *The Theology of Death and Eternal Life*, Cork, 1971.

THOMPSON W., "The Doctrine of Hell", *The Ecumenist*, 10(1972)33-37.

TILLICH P., *Systematic Theology III, Life in the Spirit, History and the Kingdom of God*, Chicago, 1963, pp. 409-418.

WALKER D. P., *The Decline of Hell*, London, 1964.

INDEX

For Scripture texts and central topics consult *Contents*.
Below is given a list of authors and some important topics.